THE LORD WILL PROVIDE

How to position yourself
to receive God's blessings

Kevin Luke

Kevin Luke

The Lord Will Provide/ Kevin Luke. – 2nd ed.
ISBN 978-1495331404

When I wrote and published the first edition of this book I was still coming out of a deep depression after the loss of my family, home, and business. Not long after submitting this book for printing my computer crashed and I had no funds for a new one to improve my book. A year later, a good friend of mine, Steve Higgins gave me a computer, and I have now updated this book with more information and better editing. Please enjoy and thank you for purchasing a copy.

There are so many people I have met in life who have inspired me and contributed to what I wrote in this book. Among those people are Diane, Tanya, Karen, my father and my two brothers, and many mentors such as Jim Borgman and Steve Pathman.

Special thanks goes out to my friend Amy Gonzalez who I went to grade school and high school with. It was after meeting at our class reunion and subsequent discussions that I felt motivated to write. Amy also provided further help in reading and giving me recommendations while writing this book, along with my other test readers Michael and Lynette.

This was also written for my kids, Nicholas and Zachary, the joys of my life.

CONTENTS

PART THREE
THE LORD DOES WHAT IS RIGHT FOR US

Introduction

Where are you going? Where have you been? Are you where you believed you would be at this point in your life, and if not, why? You only have one life; you can do as you please. You make choices every day; you make choices that affect where you are now and where you will be in the future. In this life there are many ups and downs, good times and bad. Each day presents its own challenges. How have you met these challenges? How have the challenges and difficulties of each new day affected you? Each day's challenges and difficulties change and mold you into what you are and what you will be. The difficulties and your reaction and how you meet those difficulties not only have an effect on you, but on others around you. This can be for your benefit and the benefit of others or it can be to your detriment and/or the detriment of others. Your reaction to each day's new challenges will determine your future and what direction you will take in your life.

My name is Kevin and at this point in my life I'm part of the class called the working poor. In 2013 I made about $15,000.00 working a part time job. I have paid about 41% of that income to my ex-wife for child support and to help cover additional expenses for my two boys. Because my kids do not live with me, I do not qualify for any kind of government assistance to help me though this period of my life. I mostly survive on the charity of others. It was not always this way; I had it all at one time. I will go into this later in this book. I am sharing my story in an attempt to pass on a little knowledge to help you though your journey in life.

As I have reached middle age and as I look back at my life, I understand how fast life goes and see how I have changed. I have had many ups, downs, and gone through many difficult times. Some of the challenges and difficulties I have met head on, others crushed me under their weight. I see how they have affected me, and have made me who I am today.

It is said that there is nothing as consistent as change; change takes place all the time. What we go through at each new day will make us different than what we were the day prior. Each day in one's life is a new beginning with its own blessings and challenges.

Looking back on my life, I can see where the Lord has been there for me, to assist me and guide me. There were times when I accepted His help and guidance, and other times when I did not accept the direction that He had laid out for me. Because of this I suffered the consequences of my actions. There were times when others have been there to help, to lead, and guide me through the difficult times. There were times when I knew how to proceed and my subconscious has been there telling me, warning me to slow down, stop, and think about what I was doing.

I have learned much over the years and I would like to share those experiences with you. I have made countless mistakes, reacted poorly to problems, and reacted positively to other problems. There has been much joy and happiness in my life, likewise there has also been much pain and sorrow. I write this in an effort to show you what I have done wrong so you will not make the same mistakes. I will be happy if what I write in this book can assist you in the challenges that you are facing or soon may go through. Please read, take to heart what I tell you in the coming pages, learn, or just set it aside; that is your choice, but please do not make the same mistakes that I have made.

We cannot consistently dwell on the regret of our choices or what we had to live through in our past. The past cannot be changed, it is what it is, and it made us what we are today. All we can hope for is to have a brighter future. Our future is determined not as much by our choices from the past, but from the choices and decisions that we make today and in the coming days. We need to look forward to each new day and plan for tomorrow. If we do that we will have a clear vision of what we are doing, of where we are going, and make tomorrow's choices better than today's.

Now let's get started on your bright new future.

Have you ever asked yourself these questions?

- Why is life so hard?
- Why is it that things go well just before my life falls apart once again?
- If God is so great why does He never help me?
- Why do I go through so much trouble in my life?
- Why don't things get any better? Same garbage, different day. No matter how hard I work and try I just keep sinking into the depths of despair and sorrow.
- Why, why, WHY?

I have asked myself questions such as these and many more from time to time in my life; I'm sure that many of you have as well.

PART ONE

HOW WE MESS
UP OUR LIVES

CHAPTER ONE

SOMETIMES LIFE SUCKS

When despair came into my life it hit me like a ton of bricks and I wanted to do whatever I could to get away from my troubles. The emotional pain seemed unbearable and it haunted me day and night. I tried to do things that I never would have dreamed of before I fell into the abyss of misery. I knew it was coming and it was like the perfect storm; I saw my life spiraling out of control but I felt like there was nothing I could do to stop it.

As the despair continued, I entered into a sadness which quickly grew into a depression and I began to feel sorry for myself and my situation. I saw no way out and I believed that things would never change, would never get any better. I questioned my life, my faith and my decisions, including every choice and decision that I had ever made. It came to the point where fear entered my heart. I was afraid of making any kind of decision, even the smallest of decisions became impossible without doubt entering my mind, wondering if this could be the right choice or will this just bring more pain and sorrow.

Because of my belief in God, I wondered, "Why is he doing this to me? He can make things better, He can work things in my favor, and I have always believed in Him, why can he not help, even just a little bit, so I can make it through all this? Does He not hear my prayers? Does He not love me? What is God's purpose for all of this?"

The cry came so often, "Please help me Loving Lord and Heavenly Father, please help; I'm at the end of my rope and I cannot take anymore!" Then I wondered, "Why does He not help?" "I need you Lord more than ever in my life, please help!"

I prayed and things almost started getting better, but then I was hit again and again by more problems, more loss, more pain and despair. It shook my whole belief structure to its core as it continued on. Hours turned into days, which turned into weeks, months and at times years, and I saw nothing better on the horizon. As this went on, I became more inward focused, as everything around me that I cared about what gone and all that was left was just pain and despair.

"Please help me, please!"

This was my experience although it was far from where I started in life. In 2006 I felt that I had finally hit the pinnacle of success after years of struggle. I had a great wife and two young boys. We lived in a 3,600 square foot, two story 4 bedroom semi-custom built home that we had just purchased two years before, with a three car garage, on almost two acres of land, on a corner lot in an upper middle class neighborhood. I was finally finding more success in my commercial real estate business that I had owned since 2001. That year I made $200,000.00 by myself. When my wife went back to work full time once our two boys were in school that brought our household income up to over $260,000.00.

I was on top of the world; life was great. When I went grocery shopping I would try to get the best, healthiest organic food. It was of no concern that I paid twice as much; I had the money and believed it was worth it. That year we also invested in landscaping. My wife and I did it ourselves, she laid out the landscape plan and I did most of the work. She helped where she could. I like doing work like that. Working with my hands brings me back to my youth when I worked as a landscaper for a while along with a wide variety of other jobs. I put about $30,000.00 into black dirt, flowers, bushes and trees for the front and sides of our home.

Things were good, life was good, and my wife and I were working alongside one another, working together to improve our home and our lives. There is something special when you can work alongside your spouse in such a fashion, it brings you closer. Our problems and difficulties of the past were forgotten and we were moving on together.

In reality, while I was planting the bushes in front of my home, I was actually sowing the seeds of my own doom and destruction. It is not like I did not know that all of this could lead to problems, but I relegate it to the back of my mind and made myself think that it would all work out.

I had actually begun sowing these seeds a few years before when we decided to sell our first home and find a newer, bigger one. When we got married in 1995, my income was up and down. We struggled, but slowly things had become better, we had a home that we could afford, but that was not enough.

We purchased our first home the summer of 2000, the same year that my second son was born. It was a good home, one that we could afford since I was the sole bread winner in the house. Over the next few years we redecorated it, and fenced in the yard for the yellow dog, as my oldest son called it. The dog was a yellow Lab. My oldest son, who was born in 1998, loved the color yellow and he wanted a yellow dog. The dog made him so happy, they were inseparable

We did further renovation work on the home, put in a new window, completely redecorated the kitchen, and painted and wallpapered the entire home. We had finally made it ours and put our mark on it. My wife had amazing decorating talent. We must have put close to $30,000.00 into the house. I thought that we would stay there for at least a while; it was good. However, within a couple of years my wife decided that she wanted a new home. I resisted at first because I was nervous about increasing our expenses. She worked on me, as wives often do, and eventually I gave in.

This was 2004, and we had only lived in our first home since 2000. We went out looking for a new home. My wife would have been satisfied with a band new house, one moderately better than the one that we had, but I wanted to go all out. The housing market was still in the boom phase and my business was expanding, so I wanted to get the best that we could afford, or that I made myself believe we could afford.

We put our house on the market, and I went out and found our dream home. As dreams sometimes are, it was not based on reality. I knew it would be a struggle for a few years but I got one of those interest only mortgages which the banks were pushing at the time, and I thought that I could afford it. I also knew that my wife would be returning to work in a few years, and the added income would see us though any slow times in my business.

My wife questioned me on the affordability of this grand home but I promised her that we could afford it. She even warned me that if we lost it, she would divorce me. To be truthful, I was a bit concerned as well. I prayed and asked God to guide me, "Is this the right decision?" I prayed that if this was the wrong choice that things would not work out in purchasing this house. Well He did try to warn me, and put obstacles in my way. Did I listen? No I did not!

I was so focused on this new home and so enthralled with my own abilities and the status that I would attain with this house that I closed my eyes to the warning signs. All the while I told my wife things would work out. Every obstacle the Lord put in our path, I relied on my own abilities and intellect to get around. I wanted this and there was nothing that anyone could do to stop me. I was so proud of myself that I had almost scammed my way into this new great house. All we needed to do was buy it and all else would be good.

I had taken over the business that my father had built in 2001, as his health slowly declined. It gave me a sense of accomplishment. I began thinking of myself as this big captain of industry, someone of power and importance. Income in real estate is up and down, but I was in a position that I could draw money out of the company to help carry me through the slow times in my own earnings and did not set much aside for the slow economic periods. Things were improving; the market was on a boom phase after the 1998 mild recession. I thought that the good times would continue.

I had let my arrogance get the better of me, thinking that all would work out as it had in the past for me. I had a plan all laid out concerning how we would afford such a lavish home and lifestyle. Things were all going to work out, they always had, and I believed that they would in the future.

After my best year in 2006, my income steadily dropped along with the economy. I was not fully open with my wife as to how bad things were getting. I knew that if I was, it would be a huge argument, ending with her leaving with the kids. I hoped that things would soon turn around. All I needed was one or two good deals at work and we would be back on top again. To see us through I borrowed money. I had every intention of paying it all back, whenever that one good deal came in.

By 2009, the market was on a steep decline and it all came to a head in June 2010. I earned one last commission at my business which enabled me to pay my bills up to date, except my mortgage was a month behind, it had been running that way for a while. That was it. No more money came from my business. I had already spent the few reserves that I had, I had cashed out my whole life insurance policy that I had purchased years before, and the house went into foreclosure, as many others did that year.

With no money coming in from my business, my wife pushed me into getting a part-time job. I resisted this at first because I knew that if I did, I could not focus on the real estate business, and I just knew that something was going to come in. I would get the next big money maker and things would be good. As the bills piled up and customers dropped off in real estate I did eventually get two part-time jobs to try to make ends meet, but it was not enough. I worked my two part-time jobs while trying to run the real estate business, but it did not work, and I lost my business. In November 2010 my wife announced that she wanted a divorce and before I knew it I was in the middle of my own perfect storm.

The storm continued. Every time I believed that I had reached the bottom and things would begin to pick up, it all came crashing down once again. The winter and early spring of 2011 I had one last deal that I was working on at my business. I was tired because I was working day and night between the three jobs, putting in 70 hours or more a week. I had a big potential sale taking place and if it worked out I could get my house out of foreclosure or get a new home that we could afford. If this worked, all would be good once again, or so I hoped.

Like everything else this last great deal blew apart. After I had spent hours and hours working and nursing it along, it was gone, along with any hope of saving my marriage, home, and business. In June 2011 my wife moved out of the home with the kids, leaving me in an almost empty house, with no bed, just a television, a few dishes, my computer, and a chair, along with a bunch of stuff that we had gathered over the years that she did not want or could not fit into her new place.

I slept on an air mattress, and sat in the chair and watched TV when I wasn't working. My only companions were one of our two dogs, a cat that I had given my wife a few years before and a rabbit that we had purchased for my sons at the county fair.

In February 2012, the house was finally sold via a short sale, and I found myself, at 47 years old moving back into my parental home with my mother, working two jobs and had $100,000.00 in debt, most of that to the IRS. The IRS debt was a huge factor in losing my marriage, I think even bigger than losing the house. If it were just losing the house, my wife would have stayed, but the two combined was way too much. In 2006, when I earned all that money I paid off every debt that I had, every credit card and every loan, and I was free and clear. What I neglected to do was set money aside for the government, instead, I put it into the house. My banker friend warned me but did I listen? Again, the answer is no. I felt that I knew better, that I could use this money to improve the house and pay the government off from the next deal. Well that was not to happen. I had come full circle in my life back to where it had all begun, I had almost nothing and I was living off the kindness of others.

This had not been the first time that my life had been blown apart, but it was by far the worst. As I have said, things mostly worked out for me in my life, in one way or the other. The Lord had set things up for my success in life. I was given a business by my father, I had a great wife and children, and my first home was good, in a nice neighborhood. I was not satisfied, and wanted more. I thought that I deserved more in my life. I was impatient and wanted it all now, rather than waiting and letting those things come naturally, according to the Lord's will.

If I would have let things be for a few more years and followed the guidance of the Lord, rather than going my own way, things would have been so different. If we had stayed in our first home that we had put so much money into fixing up, in 2006, I would not have had so many bills to pay off with my earnings that year. I would not have put all that money into landscaping; I could have paid my taxes as well as paid off my house. My life would be so different.

It is now February 2015, almost three years to the day that I first moved back into my mother's home. Although my situation has not improved much, the drastic free fall has ended, or at least I hope so. I can now look on my situation from a new, different perspective. I have learned so much, I have grown as a person both in a natural basis and a spiritual one.

The majority of this book was written during the winter of 2013, when I had finally started coming out of my depression over the loss of those things that I held so near and dear, including my wife who I felt was my soul mate for life, and my kids whom I love more than anything else in this world, and the way things once were. It shows what I was just beginning to understand about life, and about God. I began to understand that things were working for my own benefit, even though I couldn't see it at the time.

I learned that we need to pry all worry and concern from our lives, and put it all into Gods hands, for we can do nothing by worrying, no matter how hard we try. What we do out of our own mind and will ends in disaster. He does what is right and best and is the only one that can change things for the better. We can do nothing except follow His guidance and rely on Him.

CHAPTER TWO

MY STORY

I was born into a middle class family, the youngest of three boys. I guess you could say that I was the accident; I'm 12 years younger than my closest brother. I had a good youth, especially being so much younger, as my parents, as older parents often are, were more established financially than they were when my older siblings were born.

I grew up in an almost rural community, though we were not that far away from suburban Chicago, at the time that I was growing up. Except for the 1.5 square mile development that we lived in, it was all farms and corn fields. It was great country life, only 20 minutes from "town" as we called it.

I had a great group of friends in the neighborhood while growing up, and it seemed like they were always looking out for me. We would spend our summers running through the woods across the street from my house or going through the corn fields or swamps, just having fun, and enjoying life. In the winter we would build snow forts and have snow ball fights or go to the pond in the middle of the woods to go ice skating. It was a great childhood, a great time to grow up. There were no cares or worries in life. We had none of the problems that there is today with guns and violence.

The other aspect of my life was church. I came from a religious household; my father was a minister in our church. We belong to the New Apostolic Church, it is more than just one congregation, and it is a world-wide group of members that are almost like immediate friends or even family. No matter where you go in the world, if you get together with other New Apostolics, they will open their home to you and treat you like they have known you their whole life.

We were constantly getting together with other members from the church both from our congregation and other congregations from around the Chicago area. Here I had a whole separate and distinct friend structure in my life, full of others who I had fun with, learned from, and who watched out for me.

The church has a strong youth organization, and as I grew into my teen years I became a member of it. Through this my friend circle expanded even more with people my own age from the area, some I knew from my childhood years, but also from other areas in the United States, Canada and around the world.

In those days the church's youth organization was a little different than it is today. Back then we had our Confirmation at age 15, and at that point we no longer went to Sunday school, and we entered the youth group. Most stayed as a part of the youth group from Confirmation until they were married. This provided for a wide range of ages as part of the group. We had those in their young teens on up to those in their twenties and some beyond. While we had a disparity in age which is not always a good thing, we also had a group of more experienced, mature members that would be there to serve as mentors and guides for the younger ones. The older ones often looked out for the younger ones.

This is where my friend Jim Borgman came into my life. He kind of knew me and when I was 15 he was in his early 20's and took me under his wing to help me through the tough teen years. He was a good friend and we built a good bond, although I did scratch his new car up one evening.

The years in youth group were a time of deep religious teaching mixed in with more casual fun activities. Once a month we would have an evening of religious discussion, and on another night we had a youth choir practice, we also had a monthly get together at each other's houses and at the end of the month we had a special church service for the youth group.

Once or twice a year we would also have youth gatherings with other youth groups that came from different areas of the country. Often times, being from the Chicago area, we would get together with the youth groups from Indiana, Michigan, Detroit or even St Louis. We took trips to Denver and Texas as well. The big event for the year was every August, when all the youth from across the United States and Canada would gather in Kitchener, Canada for a big youth weekend and church service on Sunday before returning home. The members in South Eastern Canada, and Detroit would open their homes so we all would have a place to sleep and eat when not at the youth events. We had some good, happy times back then. I was able to meet and learn from many different people in that lived in diverse circumstances.

I think the highlight of my life was when I was 19. A call went out that they needed volunteers to help build churches in the Samoan Islands. We were there for about two weeks; it was a great experience to be exposed to new cultures. I was the youngest and they nicknamed me Gilligan, after the T.V. show Gilligan's Island, and of course there was another guy that we called Skipper.

All of the things I learned and relationships that I had built during those years served as a foundation for my future life. They also gave me the knowledge, strength, and experience that I needed to guide me though the rest of my life. There were many times that I drew on this while I was going through my troubles of the last few years.

Everything serves a purpose in God's plan. He will give us what we need to make it through our dark days. He helps us at all times, though we may not always see or recognize it at the time.

I have had many problems in my life as well as well as many good experiences. When I reached my mid-twenties things began to fall apart. I was almost killed in a car accident and was in a coma with multiple fractures. I was hospitalized for a month and in rehab for two months after that. I also got engaged to marry someone too soon, and two months before the wedding my fiancé called it off. She told me the proverbial, "I love you but I'm not in love with you."

The breakup of my first engagement threw me into the first great depression of my life. I was left deep in debt since we had run up my credit cards to pay for the wedding, book the reception hall, and get things ready. She lived far away, so when she moved to where I was, I rented her an apartment. I also purchased furniture for our living room so we could make plans and get ready for our lives after the wedding. Our plan was that she would find a job and we would use the cash from the wedding to pay off our debts. Once we broke up, of course this was not to be.

When we broke up I was left with a huge pile of debt, an apartment that I could not afford, and furniture that I did not need. This was all in addition to trying to get over the loss of a girl that I thought I loved and expected to spend the rest of my life with. I found a sub-tenant for the apartment and tried to manage the debt the best that I could. In hindsight, I should have declared bankruptcy then, and gotten rid of the debt. However, if that happened, I probably would not have met my now ex-wife, which would have been a loss for me as well.

I moved on with my life, the best that I could. I renewed connections with old friends that I had grown up with and we went out and had some fun activities. I just needed to get my ex-fiancée off of my mind. I was majorly depressed; I even started smoking a little for a while, which was out of character for me because I had been an anti-smoking advocate until then. I paid for a dating service so I could meet new people. This was foolish because I was already deep in debt and it did not pan out too well, but I was working through this depression and I needed a release.

One of the ways that I decided to get over the pain and depression was to take a vacation. I booked a trip on a Caribbean cruise. This is why I said if I would have declared bankruptcy I would not have met my first wife. I just piled on the debt. I went by myself just to get away for a while and see who I would meet and gain a new perspective on life. It was on the first night of that cruise that I met my now ex-wife. The ship had not even left port yet and I spotted her.

We dated for about six months before we became engaged for the first time. I say for the first time because the night before our wedding we called it off. Our argument that night was about finances. Our wedding was on a Sunday and Monday morning we were to leave on our honeymoon in Mexico. Of course I had piled on more debt planning for this wedding. We had rented an apartment and I had again purchased furniture. We had already booked and paid for our honeymoon, and the question was what we were going to do with the money gifts from the wedding.

We had done much to get ready, but had not opened a joint bank account. She did not have a bank account, so I thought that we should deposit the money into my bank account before we left, and we could then transfer it into a joint account when we returned. She did not want that; she was fearful that I would use that money to pay off my debt from my first engagement. Her idea was to give the money to her mother to deposit into her account and then open a new account upon our return. I did not agree with that. That was our impasse and we broke up.

The next morning my father, two brothers, my nephew and I rented a truck and went down to the apartment to get my stuff out of there, including the furniture that I had purchased. I now had a second set of furniture to get rid of in just over two years' time.

This is an example of how one problem can lead to another and another after that.

Of course we got back together and eventually got married. Before my first son was born in February 1998, my wife and I got into an argument and she moved out. Her and her family came and took most of the items from our apartment and I was left with a television and a few things, much the same as I was when the house was foreclosed on. It is actually the same television! So I purchased a third set of furniture.

We had a couple of great boys, and we had our problems, mostly caused by finances. I eventually did declare bankruptcy, and got my debt situation straightened out. My income though was up and down, as I was in a commission-based business. I went through cycles of debt and paying bills down, not always off. I was also kind of free and loose with my money.

As I got older, the scars from my past started to affect the present. As I grew out of my financial problems and began to make more and more money, I tried to overcompensate for my financial deficiencies from the first couple years of our marriage, and I started to spend more and more in an effort to make sure that my wife and kids were happy and did not lack for anything. I went from being in debt to getting out of it and then back into it again.

CHAPTER THREE

WHY DO BAD THINGS KEEP HAPPENING TO ME?

This is a question that I'm sure we have all asked ourselves. I know I have asked myself many times. We suffer a loss, then one problem after another comes, until we can no longer see a clear path out of our situations and see no indication that things will change for the better. Why is this?

Many times when we ask this it is because we have a tendency to blame God for our conditions or situations. We also begin to make excuses for ourselves and blame others. To answer this question, we first need to look at ourselves, ask ourselves the question - what have I done and what am I still doing that has caused this to happen to me. We need to search ourselves for the answer.

When you have questions about your life, you must first look at yourself for you have control over your own life. We have the control over what we do, what we say and how we treat others. What we do, how we act and treat others, what image we want to portray to others through our words, deeds and our attitude is a main factor in how we are treated and what we have to live through in our lifetime.

We need to question ourselves about what are we doing or not doing that keeps us in the same cycle of problems. This is difficult to do because our own ego gets in the way. We have a tendency to think that what we do and what we are is good and everything is someone else's fault.

We think that we don't do anything wrong, but look at those around us and judge their actions. We often put the blame on others for our problems. It is always easier to blame others than for us to accept responsibility for our own life and actions. We convince ourselves that we have no control; that it is the fault of others, the decisions of others, how others treat us, what they could have done for us, and what they do not do for us. It is not my fault; it is because he said that or she did this.

We blame the government and any number of other things for our problems. Sometimes people say, "God has cursed me or does not love me. If there were a God, He would not allow this to happen." On the other end of the scale there are those who blame Satan for their problems, that it is a big plan of Satan to bring them down and pull them away from God. We just want to blame someone or anything else but ourselves. We make excuses for ourselves.

A minister I heard when I was growing up said that there is an old German saying about excuses and accusers. "When you make excuses for your own actions; they will come back and accuse you of your own wrong doings." Making excuses will not do anything for you in life, except keep you in your same circumstances.

Once we convince ourselves that it is not because of what we are doing, but our circumstances are caused by an outside force that we have no control over, we go back to the same old thing, the same actions, and the same mistakes and then the same things keep happening to us over and over again. Each time something bad happens we look to others rather than taking responsibility for our actions. We also look to others to fix the problems that we caused.

How can others help us in our difficulties or why should they fix our problems if we are the cause of them?

This is especially true if we refuse to recognize that the reason we are living though such problems is our own fault. Since we refuse to recognize that we are the cause of those problems and we refuse to change, that means that no matter what they do to help us or change our situation, we will always fall back into the same circumstances.

When we place all blame on others for our problems and then look to others to solve those problems, we are actually relinquishing all responsibility for our own lives to others. We will no longer have control over our lives and no chance to better our situation. All of this is because we do not want to be responsible for what has happened to us and what we are living through.

What are you doing or not doing that keeps you in the same conditions? Look at yourself, and your life, find the answer, and change. Take control of your life; it is your life, and not anyone else's. Your happiness and joy depend on you and no one else. As the saying goes, "Life is what you make it!" God put it in your hands; now what will you do with it?

This reminds me of a parable that the Lord Jesus spoke. In the parable there was a rich ruler who was going on a trip to a faraway land. Before he left he called his servants and gave each of them some money, or talents. To one he gave ten, to another five and to the third one.

When the ruler returned he asked his servants what had become of what he had given them. The first one which he gave ten talents to said that he had invested the money and gained ten more talents. To the second that he had given five talents to, likewise he had invested the money and had gained five more talents to. To these two the ruler gave much more. When he asked the third what he had done with the one talent, the servant said that he was scared to lose his master's money so he hid it and returned the one talent back to him.

This made the ruler angry because this servant did not use and increase what he had been given. So the ruler took away the one talent and gave it to the first servant who had received ten talents and cast away the servant that had only received one talent.

The Lord has given us something much more than money; He has given us life and a free will. He has also given us many abilities. What do we do with them? Do we take control and use what the Lord has given us to better ourselves and situations, or do we bury and hide what he has given us, and let others take control of our lives? It is all in our hands.

We may not like our situation, but we have to deal with it the best that we can. We should use our circumstances for our benefit and look for ways that we can improve. This reminds me of a story that I heard in Church on Sunday. There was a man in Africa who could not walk and spent his time begging at the marketplace. After a time he found that he was making less and less money so he asked someone why this was. He was told that there was now a blind man at the other end of the marketplace begging as well. Because of this, people were dividing their money among two people where there was once only one.

Of course this led to a dispute between the two beggars, let's say a turf war. This went on for a while until they realized that they were being unproductive. At this point the man who had no legs went to the blind man and said that they should work together. He would be the eyes for the blind man and the blind man could be his legs. With this the two began to work together and they could then earn money on their own without having to spend the day begging for others to help them.

These individuals had been suffering under a bad situation but were able to come together and use their abilities for their each other's benefit. Sure it was not the best of situations, but it worked for them. They looked at their situation and rather than sitting and complaining, fighting and placing blame they worked together to better themselves.

The Law of Physics states that to every action there is an equal and opposite reaction. This is a fundamental law of the universe. This does not only apply to the movement of the stars and planets in the universe, or the movement of atomic particles in the molecular world. It also applies to our everyday life, our words and deeds. Everything has an action and a reaction whether we want to realize it or not. We cannot just go through life numb to those around us, their views, and opinions and how what we do affects them and what they do affects us and our lives.

Too many times we can do or say something that will cause a reaction in others. There are some people who will do this just for fun or for spite. The thing that we do not realize is that everything we do or say will have an effect either positive or negative, not only on others but back on ourselves. People do or say things at work that cause problems without realizing that it reflects badly on them and then they wonder why they lost their job.

It can be like an atom bomb exploding. When a nuclear bomb explodes there is a force that begins a chain reaction of atoms being destroyed or split. The particles from one atom hit more atoms which in turn blow apart and so on, and then the reaction grows within a matter of milliseconds. As these atoms are blown apart it will cause destruction in a larger and larger area.

The Sun operates on the same principle, atom after atom of Hydrogen is split apart and this will continue until no more hydrogen remains. It is a self-sustaining force.

Our actions or inactions work on the same principle. We do or say something, we try to portray a certain image, we come across with a certain attitude, or we show our disgust or our own self-importance which causes a response in others, whether we intended it or not. When our actions cause a positive effect on others, then their actions will return cause a positive effect back to us. On the contrary though, if our actions caused a negative effect on others then this will reflect badly on us and cause negative effects in our lives. In turn, what we do will reflect either negatively or positively on the view that others have about us.

If others have a poor view or perspective about you due to your own actions, this will affect your life negatively. It will affect whether people are willing to help you and do things for you. It can affect whether you will get a job, get a promotion, or if you will keep your job. Everything that you do, say, or imply is important to you, your future, and family.

Our actions not only affect those in the immediate proximity, but like the atom bomb will affect others all around. The bad attitude spreads its destruction on others with no consideration. As this destruction spreads it will come back to us in ways that we never imagined. I'm sure that you have heard the adage, "what goes around, comes around." If you treated others poorly you will also be treated poorly by others. If you have hurt others you will also suffer loss or pain. It all works under the same principle, every action has an equal and opposite reaction.

I know everyone wants to be their own person, and do their own things; they do not want to listen to others but only want to go their own way. Sure that is fine, but if you want to go your own way in life, you cannot expect to gain the same rewards as those who follow the social the social norms. Some people do not understand this: they think they can look, do things, or say whatever they want. They will then complain about and blame others when life does not work out the way that they had planned or expected.

We all portray a certain image about ourselves, it goes to what groups we hang around with, how we dress, how we act around others. This all signifies us as part of one group or another, who we are and what we want others to believe we are. There are people who are so called "know it all's" that we meet. They want to portray the image that they know everything or at least more than they actually know. They have an opinion on everything, and know everything, and get angry when you tell them different. There are others who want to portray a mean, tough image that they have the world in their grasp and no one will tell them otherwise. There are those who will dress and act like they are some big gang member, because they believe it is "cool" to do so. This is if they are in a member of a street gang or not. The thing that we need to remember in life is that others will treat you according to the image that you, yourself want to portray. It is like a mirror, what gets reflected back to you, is only what you yourself show others.

This goes into the golden rule, "do unto others as you would have them do unto you." How we act around others, how we treat those around us, are key to how we want to be treated.

It is all in the seeds that you plant. A farmer cannot plant corn and expect to grow wheat. Likewise a person cannot act like they are this anti-social rebel and expect to receive all the benefits of the society. It is all about personal responsibility.

When things go wrong in life, it is important not to blame others for your problems. Look first at yourself to see what you are doing wrong; this is especially true in the area of finances. All too many times people look to spend their money on the so called "fun" things in life, their toys, or things to inflate their image. The first and foremost thing that we should use our earnings for is the support and stabilization of our family. Once that is secure, then you can look at doing the rest. What good is the latest, fastest car, if your family loses their home?

Are you one of those people who believe in signs? I will admit I am or was, I guess I still do in a way. What I'm talking about is something happens and we decide to take it as a sign that we should not move forward. Yes, this can be true, we see warnings of impending troubles and we need to realize that we are on the wrong path and we need to change course. The problem is that all of this is very subjective. We decide if a problem or difficulty is a sign or we just dismiss it as a coincidence.

Why do bad things keep happening? Why do we always end up in more problems and difficulties? Maybe it is because we are looking at the world around us as how we want it to be and not how things really are. We do not deal in reality. We become so focused on what we want that we dismiss the reality of the situation and keep moving in the wrong direction.

On the reverse I will use the example that we may not like the job that we have and unrelated problems or events happen and we take it as a sign that we should leave that job. We decide that those things were signs that we should quit this job, that a higher power wants us to quit this job because this higher power has something better for us in our future. In truth, we have quit a job we do not like and made God responsible for our decision when He had nothing to do with it. We go ahead and quit the job, have no job, no money and a world of problems that have fallen upon our shoulders. Then we wonder why. We blame God for our problems and our difficulties when He had nothing to do with them. It was our choice to leave our job. We caused these problems and now we look to God to fix them for us.

The Lord does provide paths for us to achieve success, He wants us all to be successful in life, but we need to follow His path and not go our own way. The Lord will warn us of problems and dangers, signs that we should recognize and follow, but all too often we decide not to follow these signs and we go our own way doing what we want to. Here again we blame God for not warning us and leading us different. Why do bad things keep happening? Because of the choices we make and because of the things we do.

If we do not listen to the warnings of impending danger, if we refuse to change and get back on the right course, if we keep doing the same thing, then we should expect the same results. Maybe if it hurts badly enough we will make the changes necessary to stop doing the things that cause the same bad circumstances to happen time and time again.

CHAPTER FOUR

FINANCES

Are you broke all the time? I know I am. Are you under constant harassment by bill collectors? I have deal with that as well during multiple times in my life. My debt has been cleaned up many times and I have said that I would not go back into debt just to have it happen again a few years later. None of us know what lies in our future.

We can blame it on the economy, work problems, co-workers, or competition at work or in business. There is more beyond that though. Finances are very basic, yet even the government cannot figure it out. Don't spend more than you take in. This sounds so simple but the problem is that it does not work out that way. Things are expensive, we all need and want things, our kids need and want things, and everyone wants something from us.

Added to this there are thousands out there who are willing to give us what we want; it will just cost us a little of our money. There is a whole industry dedicated to convincing us of what we want and need and the urgency to have it right now.

We just have to have the nicest house and car. Our kids must have the latest gaming system and the latest games, or maybe we want to have that latest game or system. We surely need the latest smart phone. "I don't have the money so I will just put it on the credit card and take care of it later." There are all kinds of finance options available as well, even if we cannot afford it. The financers will make it sound easy for you to pay for it. It will sound so nice and easy, "Just a few dollars a month, surely you can afford that, can't you?"

Hold on there, stop, don't do it. You may have a good job, and make okay money, but you are throwing it all away just because you have been convinced that you need that latest thing, right now. You are being charged a boatload of interest just because you could not wait. We here in America just throw our money away and then sit and cry and complain about why we are broke all the time. We will rob our future and our children's future just so we can have something that we do not really need right now.

There was once a time when people in this country saved their money. If they could not afford what they wanted or needed, they did not buy it until they saved up enough to pay for it. Then the credit industry was born and the world changed. We could get what we wanted or what we thought we needed right now and then push the responsibility off to later. While we continue pushing it off, the banks and credit card companies are making millions, draining us of our income, the fruits of our labor and our children's future.

When we build our life on credit, we our building our future and our children's future out of IOU'S, and as we have seen in recent years, this foundation is not stable and the house will come crashing down. When it comes down we lose everything.

When we build our future on credit and hope rather than on the solid planning and wise decisions, there is nothing substantial to hold it in place when problems arise and the facts of our life become apparent. This is what I did. I secured my family, my livelihood, and my entire future on a pipe dream of what I thought it could be and what I made myself believe things were. This reminds me of the parable that Jesus spoke concerning the two builders. One builder had built his house on a rock, and when the storms came, it stood strong. The other builder built his home on sand, and when the water rose and the wind came, it came crashing down.

When we build anything based on our own ideas rather than on reality it is like building a house on sand. This sand shifts and moves and changes, it is not stable. If we build our future on the rock of facts and reality, it will remain stable and not fall when the storms of life assail us.

There was once a time in this country when each generation would be better than the preceding generation. Now all we have is debt upon debt; but they have a bunch of gadgets and toys to play with. They may have the latest gaming system, and the nicest big screen television but no home to play it in.

We all want instant gratification. I know I did. I wanted the good life, that good rich image. I wanted my family to have everything that they had ever dreamed of or that I had ever dreamed of. This all worked until the economy crashed and it became apparent that what I had done was built my future on the shifting sands of dreams rather than the rock of truth and the facts. Like the house in the parable it all came crashing down for myself as the entire economic structure of the country fell apart.

Why did the economy crash? Is it because everyone was living like I was? The people, the government, the banks, and businesses all wanted instant gratification, or more money. I remember back in the 90's, when Clinton was president, the politicians in the federal government said that they wanted to make it possible for every American to own their own home, no matter what their credit status was. If they could make it look like they could pay for it, the bank should give them the loan for the new house. So the politicians loosened up the banking regulations and told the banks that they had to make these loans. The banks would make more money off of the loans and they dutifully went along with the idea. The politicians made the voters happy, the banks earned their money, houses were built and sold, people were put to work, the economy boomed, and boomed, for the next decade or so. That is when the warning signs began, little inklings of the upcoming disaster. The people did not want to recognize it, the politicians dismissed it, the banks were scared, but they already had their hand in the cookie jar. Then it all fell apart.

I wanted to have it all. I wanted the good life, not in a few years, but right now. I needed it now. I bit into the image of life that I saw on television and the movies. I did not want to deal with the truth and the facts of my situation,

I pushed it off to another day. You can only keep pushing things off for a short time, until we cannot push it off anymore. All the while that I was pushing the problems off, they were growing and getting worse, until it all exploded. My life and world were blown apart. What good is it for me to cry and complain about my situation when I caused it? Rather than looking to the past and complaining or placing the blame on the government and others, I must look at myself and see how and why I am in the state I'm in. Then I can make the necessary changes to better our lives. It is called taking responsibility or being a responsible person in all things in life.

That is how the Lord works at times. We need to learn and grow from what we experience. In the bible it states the godly virtues and attitudes that the Lord is looking for in us. It is not that God is trying to harm us, as what some say and believe. They try to blame God or others for their situation rather than looking at themselves. God gave us a free will to make our own choices.

We make our own choices, and we also deal with the consequences of those choices. The Lord through the sacrifice of Jesus Christ provided a path to forgiveness. Through this we can be forgiven for our actions but it does not remove the consequences of those actions. We cannot expect God to save us every time we go our own way by making decisions contrary to what is right or the way that He is leading us.

We often cause our own problems and we also need to learn to follow His guidance to find our way out of our problems. He tries to show us the path that we need to follow, a path of blessing, but if we decide that we do not want to follow that path then we have to live with and suffer under that decision.

It comes down to personal responsibility; you are responsible for your own life. You own your own decisions. Once we come to terms with that fact, then we can look at our life and truly see and accept the fact that we have made bad decisions. Then we can learn from our own mistakes and begin to change ourselves and better our circumstances. Then we can begin to grow.

How do you spend your hard earned money?

I was at a store a while back, and a wife was mad at her husband. They barely had enough money to feed their kids and the husband wanted to spend $50.00 on a carton of cigarettes. He wanted his cigarettes so bad that he was willing to spend what little money they had for the temporary satisfaction of his craving rather than taking care of what they really needed - food for their family.

Life is a choice between needs and wants. We need food, shelter and clothing. That should be the main focus in what we decide to spend our money on. Everything beyond that are wants. The wants are what society or businesses use to get more of our money, to make themselves rich and the rest of us poor. Remember what they do, say, and advertise is for their benefit and not for ours.

This is more than big ticket items such as the latest hottest car, but also everyday items. Do we need that case of beer or do we need to get food or pay for shelter? What kind of clothes do we purchase, the latest hottest trends and highest prices, or do we go with standard clothing?

Clothing trends have been created by the media. If someone wears clothes that do not meet the latest fashion trends or may be a bit old or worn they can be often criticized directly or behind their back. People do not realize that not everyone has enough to spend on the latest fashions, and beyond that they may not have enough to spend to wear different clothes every day. I have heard people complain about others because they notice that they wore the same clothes to work two days in a row. Now, I do not know their personal situations, but maybe they did not have enough money to purchase enough clothes to wear something different every day. Maybe their washing machine was broken and they did not have the money to repair it. I do not know but I will give them the benefit of the doubt. We should have care and consideration for others, and not put them down just to raise ourselves up.

When it comes to food we have many choices available to us. There are choices available that give us the impression that they are inexpensive, but in fact they are not. They are quick and easy and make life simple for us. We do not have to spend time in the kitchen cooking for our family, we can feed them some fast food or precooked meals to fill the hole in their stomach and we can go on and have fun in our life.

We do not consider that the "fast" food we get is actually crap, and it is very costly. Beyond the cost of the food itself, it is not healthy and will make you gain weight. Then, as so many do, they will spend even more money for a health club membership so they can lose weight once again. Then they will spend even more money on quickie diet foods that are no better, rather than making a good home cooked meal.

I guess you don't have time to cook when you have to go to the gym, or play the new gaming system or sit on social media. It is a big industry and one feeds off of the other to find more ways to get your money, your hard earned cash. What is this all for? A little instant gratification.

As an example, I have two teenage boys, who live with my ex-wife. On days that I have them I will take them out to eat. Now they do live a distance from me right now and there is not always time nor do I have the money to bring them to where I live and cook them a meal. These boys, like most teenage boys, can eat. I have found that it cost me the same to buy and make them a steak dinner as it does to take them out to the local fast food hamburger joint. Now that really shows how much we spend for low quality fast food. The food we get at these fast food places is really bad; we just do not realize how bad it is. We have just become accustomed to low quality food that fills our stomach.

So again, where do we choose to spend our money?

We should budget and focus our time and money on what matters most and what we need most, not just on things that may bring us temporary pleasure. Don't get me wrong, there is nothing wrong with having a nice home, a nice car and all the toys we want. We have to make sure that we can afford what we want before we splurge on such items.

Affording to buy something does not mean that we can make the minimum payments on the credit card or loan. It means being able to pay cash for the item without taking away from what we need to live.

Why do bad things keep happening to you? Why don't you have the money that you need, to feed your family, to buy the things you want? Where are you spending your money? Is your situation caused by your own actions and choices? Remember, the first step in changing the world is changing you.

CHAPTER FIVE

CHANGE YOUR THINKING

We have dealt with one end of the financial equation, the outflow of cash; we need to deal with the inflow of cash. I know it is a tough job market; there are many who have lost their jobs and have taken on part-time jobs at a lower wage or have no job at all. Just what do we do in this situation? Do we get down and depressed and say that there is no use, the job market is bad, why even take the time to look for the kind of job we want? It is so easy to just sit around on the couch and watch television and set our problems aside for a while and get lost in a dream land of the Hollywood writers. T.V is like a drug; it lets us escape for a time and not deal with reality. The danger of getting lost in the habit of sitting and watching television rather than dealing with your problems is that it gives you a false sense of reality, of how things are in the world and how it operates. As my father told me when I was growing up, "T.V. will rot your brain."

Are you sitting there thinking that there are no jobs that will fit you? Maybe you have tried to find a job, went to all the job boards, checked around and found nothing good so you are ready to give up. I've been there! Even if you have applied and got nothing, do not stop, keep looking. Maybe you need to think outside the box and try something different, something you never considered. It may open up a whole new world of opportunities.

So what can you do when you are not bringing in enough cash? There is only one thing to do - work and earn more money. Sounds simple right?

I know things are hard, life is hard, but do not make excuses about why you cannot find a job or make more money. If you are having problems finding a job, maybe you need to expand your search, look elsewhere. Look at opportunities that you never thought of before or that you may think is beneath you. Do not limit yourself just so you can sit around and fool yourself by saying I can't, things are bad, the economy is bad. There is work out there, you just have to get up and find it.

I have told you about my work situation, but I have not just sat back; I have taken action to find new ways to expand my cash flow. Not all have worked as planned, but at least I'm trying. I wrote a blog for a while, I have this book and I have a second planned. An old friend from high school contacted me, named Joe Runnion who knew of my situation, and gave me advice on how to get into the business of selling on eBay. So I'm dabbling a little with that. I started trash-picking and looking for items to sell on eBay, and got into the scrapping business as well. Between what I picked up and what I found lying around in our basement, the garage and the barn, I have made a few hundred dollars. Every little bit helps, except thinking that certain jobs are beneath you. There is much that you will do when you are hungry or your kids need clothes and your car needs repair.

During the great depression my grandfather had a job the whole time. He did not sit around and say "I can't," he had a family to take care of. He went out and looked. He knocked on doors, went into businesses and asked for a job. He went into a milk company even though they had a sign out front saying, "No help wanted." He still went in and asked for a job, impressed the owner and got a job as a milkman. Just do it; ask, look, and work for it. Do not let the preconceptions of others or of yourself stop you from finding work for yourself so you can support yourself and your family.

The Lord will set opportunities before us, all we need to do is follow His way and listen to His voice. We cannot let our own preconceptions stop us from following His lead. When I think of all the money that I lost before by throwing stuff out and letting other scrappers take the stuff away because I thought that doing this was beneath me, I could kick myself.

I actually got into scrapping one day when I was mowing the lawn. It was not long after I had spoken to Joe, and I was thinking about items that I could sell on EBay. Our family has stored things in and behind the barn in my backyard for decades. Most of the stuff has been forgotten for years.

While I was cutting grass one Saturday, I spotted something in the weeds behind the barn and I got off the mower to see if it was something I could sell. When I checked it out, I found that it would not be good for that, but I looked around and saw big iron pipes that someone had put back there 40 years ago or so. I thought wow; I can scrap those and make some money. As I looked around I saw more and more scrap lying around. I hurried and finished cutting the grass, and after putting everything away I went inside and called around to see where a scrap metal place was and if they were open. I found one that would be open for a couple more hours.

I immediately went outside, drove my old banged up Mercury Mariner back by the barn and loaded up all that I could find. It took me about an hour. I drove 10 minutes to the scrap yard, unloaded the stuff and walked away with $60.00; not bad for a couple hours of work on a Saturday.

Every Saturday over the next five weeks I was digging in the barn or searching the basement and taking trips to the scrap yard. I would also go out and do a bit of trash picking and was able to grab a few items. In the end, before winter hit I was able to bring in enough money to stabilize my income for a while.

When my business was going down I went out and found part-time employment. I sucked up my pride and went to work as a cashier in a big box retail store. At the same time, I got a part-time job where I worked overnight. At this point I tried to keep my business open while working two part-time jobs. I did all I could to keep my house and my family, but it ended up being too little too late. Maybe if I would have done this a few months before, things would have turned out different.

What I did then, though it did not fix the situation, laid the foundation for my future growth and success. The Lord was blessing me but I could not see it at the time. I could have sat back and questioned why I was losing everything and why He did not seem to be helping me keep what I had. The thing is I was losing everything because of my own actions, my own choices, my own ego and stupidity. The Lord will not save us from ourselves all the time. If He stepped in to save us from ourselves every time that we screwed up we would not learn and just keep on making the same mistakes time after time.

CHAPTER SIX

ATTITUDE

One of the greatest factors that can affect your life, determining whether you find success or collapse under the weight of your problems and difficulties is your attitude. What do others see when they look at you, when they when they are around you? Even more, what do others hear when you talk? What is your perspective when you face problems? Do you use the difficulties as opportunities to grow to become a greater version of yourself, or do you let those difficulties get you down and drag you into the dirt? What is your attitude?

We all have heard the phrase, your altitude depends on your attitude. This quote is very true, more often than we believe. How do you view people when they correct you and try to give you advice? Often people are just trying to help; so listen to what they tell you, then look at yourself and see if what they are telling you applies.

How you interact with others has a lot to do with how other people perceive you, and can affect your success or failure. Have you ever met someone who comes across angry at the world? You say something to them and you get an immediate response of anger, or they immediately challenge what you say. It seems that they want to argue all the time. When they enter a room you can just see on their face that they do not want to be there, they despise the mere fact that they are there and they despise and look down on all of those around them. I have seen this and I'm sure that you have as well.

Why is this? Why are some people so into themselves that they feel that they are better than anyone and everything else and that others do not matter? We don't start out this way when we are born, but life can be hard, full of disappointments and struggles. We get cheated, lied to, and lose trust in others. However, not everyone comes out angry and closed off from the world. The difference is our reaction to the negative experiences in our life.

I think to some degree we all can gain the tendencies that I described above. Yes, some can become that way because they are spoiled as kids and believe that they are the only ones who matter in the world. Others have just been hurt so badly that they withdraw into themselves as protection from the outside. Others are beat down so much that it becomes an awful cycle of problems and as we withdraw, our attitude and perspective only causes us more and more problems.

I have seen this in others, and in myself. At times there is only so much one can take before it starts to affect you, it is not just one thing but one thing after another and another. As we grow we can be put down and teased by other kids. I experienced this like many others. This causes some to become introverted or in some cases the child lashes out at others. Little things happen and they just build up over time.

As a child I had a slight speech impediment, and was a bit withdrawn as I grew. I did not stand up for myself, and because of this for a few years during elementary school I was teased to no end by other boys in my class. This of course caused me to become more introverted. As most kids you can grow out of this as you mature in life and put it behind you, or so you think. However, it still lurks in the back of your mind. As we grow and live other problems arise and we deal with them the best that we can. Some issues are greater than others and have different effects on our personality.

As I have experienced difficulty after difficulty in my life, I became more introverted and there grew an underlying anger or hurt and distrust of others. One thing led to another and created a wide array of problems.

Especially after the purchase of our second home I was under a huge amount of stress trying to pay for it. At times I would be asked a question and would answer it, but others took it that I was angry or yelling at them. I did not comprehend this at the time, but now looking back I understand what they saw in me and my actions. Of course I did not want to see or understand what they were telling me when it was happening. This caused more problems for me at my work and in relationships.

The stress of trying to pay for a home that I could not afford coupled with my up and down income and my poor spending habits added to the stress in my marriage. The foundation for all of this had already been laid years before with the breakup of my first engagement. The stress was only increased with the U.S. economic collapse in the housing market in 2008-2009. My income as a real estate broker went down and more stress was added. This all increased the fear that I would lose my home because I could not pay for it, especially with my income slowly decreasing. I was able to carry it for a while, but the time came where I could no longer borrow the money or earn enough to keep myself afloat.

As one customer after another in my business decided not to move ahead with buying new properties my hopes and dreams died. This led to more stress at home and as problems surmounted I began to feel helpless and a failure. I did not know where to turn or what to do. With all of this going on, my business down, no new customers and those that I had disappearing, I did the exact wrong thing. Because I did not know what to do, early on, I did nothing. I would leave work early and go home and swim in our pool.

I think by this point I knew what would happen when the final day of full personal economic collapse came and we would lose our home. I knew that my marriage would come to an end and I would lose my family. Deep down inside, I wanted to spend as much time with them as I could before this happened.

It was not until after we received the foreclosure papers that I decided to find a new job. That was when I got the two part time jobs. The stress that I was going through was still unbelievable. I received the papers in September of 2010; I got the part time jobs finally in October. In November my wife said that she was thinking about a divorce. This served to increase my stress even more. As this stress grew, I eventually blew up at my family and then she said that she decided to divorce me and that was final. I spent months trying to repair the situation but to no avail.

We put our house on the market for a short sale and stayed there until she moved out in June of 2011. Our divorce was finalized a few months later. I stayed in the house, by myself. It was almost empty; she had taken almost everything with her. I slept on air mattresses on the bedroom floor until the house was finally sold in late February of 2012.

When I moved out of the house I had nothing, I could afford nothing. I moved back into my parents' home in my old room and tried to rebuild my life once again. I had lost my family, home, and business in just a few months, I was majorly depressed. I was living my life by just going through the motions, like a robot. I really did not start coming out of this until the fall of 2013 and early 2014. It was the end of 2013 that I first started writing this book.

My reaction or my attitude towards what I had experienced was off base; I see this now and understand. The problem is that I obtained understanding too late to help me in my marriage, my business, and my home. I did learn from this though so I would not make the same mistakes again in the future.

Many do not come to this realization and their attitudes keep affecting their lives in a negative way. We all need to take a good look at ourselves and see how our attitudes are affecting our chances for success and a bright future.

What is your attitude? Now be honest, everyone else sees it why don't you? People watch us, everything we do, everything that we say or write. This is especially true when it comes to work or business. People want to know what we are made of, if we are trustworthy, if they can trust us with their business or what work or job they have

Either on a business level or on a personal level, people want to know who and what they are dealing with. Can they trust you, will you be there when they need you? Will you be a help or will you and your attitude be a hindrance to them or to their business?

Just remember everyone is watching. It is not just about you in this life, it is also about all those around you, who you meet, who you are friends with and your family. As the Lord Jesus said, "Love your neighbor as you Love yourself."

When one is going through difficulties in their life, it is easy to look at others and what they have and wonder why you do not have it. This is a jealousy. We cannot be jealous of others or of what they have. I know that I have gone through this, it is basic human nature. When you have lost it all, like I have, you see people, family friends who have things that you want. A nice home, loving wife, they can live with and spend time with their kids. I have sometimes looked at my life and seen all that was missing and asked myself "Why? Why can't I have what they have? Why can't I spend time with and take vacations with my family? I do not have the funds to take any kind of vacation, and they are flying off to all parts of the world."

This will eat away at you, even in its mildest form. If jealousy is given the opportunity to grow within your heart, it can destroy families and friendships. Out of jealousy comes anger and hatred, and things can be said that only hurt and destroy. Once said, there is no taking the words of hurt and anger back.

What is your attitude? Do you cry and complain about things in life? Are you negative about the future and about life in general? Or do you look at each new day as a blessing granted unto us by God? Each new day is another fresh opportunity for each of us to achieve greatness in our lives. Do you meet people in the morning with a smile and a hearty good morning, or a frown and a grunt?

People shy away from negative people. We need to be happy be upbeat, even in the face of overwhelming problems. If you are positive about life, good things will come your way. If you are negative, all you will get are more reasons why your life is so bad.

CHAPTER SEVEN

PRIDE

Back in the days when I owned my successful business, I lived in a 3,600 Sq. Ft. house on almost two acres, had a great wife and two great sons that lived with me, and I felt like I ruled the world. This of course was in my own mind. What a change in my life from those days. I was an assistant scout master for my sons' Cub Scout troop, I could come home from work and take a dip in the pool in the back yard. Everything looked good but it was all a façade. I thought we had it all and it would continue, but it was not to be. Like a house of cards it all came crashing down around me. It was not constructed on a firm foundation, but on ego and pride.

As it is said, pride comes before the fall. I know this from personal experience. When I was making good money at my business, one day I was at a big box retail store purchasing some items and as I was checking out, I conversed with the young man who was running the register and I wondered, "Why is he doing a job such as this?" He sounded like he was smart and had something going for him, and here he was earning low wages in what I believed was a low level job. Surely there was something better that he could do for work than this. I was very prideful to the point of looking down on others who did not appear to be as successful as I had been at that time. This is the wrong attitude.

Little did I know that within a year I would be working at that same big box retail store. The person that I was looking down upon would be training me for my position. We don't always know our own future or where circumstances will place us. Likewise, we do not know the conditions and situations that others live with and why they do the things that they do.

Being prideful goes hand in hand with being judgmental, both are negative attitudes in the eyes of God. If we are unrepentant of these attitudes we will be knocked back and knocked down in our life. I know because I was very prideful and I was knocked way back. The other danger is that we begin to depend on and have faith in ourselves and in our own abilities, not in the power of God. This causes us to leave no room for God or for those around us who could give us useful information and help guide us through the turmoil in life.

My pride led me to believe that I could do anything and that I was so great that I could not fail. That is a dangerous attitude which put me into a dangerous position. I did not have a clear view of the dangers and problems that stood before me and I began to take risks and make decisions that were based on a view that I could not fail.

I'm indispensable, I'm better than anyone else.

A subset of pride is the thought that you are indispensable; that your business or job cannot go on without you. There is no one who is indispensable; you can be replaced by someone or something else. There are plenty of people waiting to take your job if you make a misstep or misjudgment.

Once you begin to believe that you are indispensable, you will begin to take things for granted and begin to take chances with your job, your family and your life, because you believe that you are safe from any retribution. When this happens you make mistakes and will suffer loss in life.

Self-Righteousness

Hand in hand with pride comes self-righteousness, the thinking that you are always right and everyone else is wrong, that you are better than everyone else. My high school drama teacher described it as the attitude of "I'm okay, and you suck." This attitude permeates our society today.

People think that they know it all and no one else can have any opinions or ideas that are worth listening to or even talking about. We even find this within Christianity; people call themselves Christians, but then stand as a judge over everyone else who does not think or believe as they do. The fact is that the only one true Judge is the Lord God. This reminds me of a quote from the Bible, from the book of Revelation. The church of Laodicea believed that because they were rich and increased with goods that they had need of nothing, but they were really naked, miserable, and poor. It is easy to think that the Lord was speaking of natural wealth here, but in fact, the Lord was speaking to the state of Christianity at that time. Today there are still too many who stand up as Judges over others, who think that they have salvation wrapped up and that if you do not believe as they do you are heading on the fast track to hell. This type of Christian thinks that they are spiritually rich and have need of nothing.

When one is self-righteous they close themselves off to others as well as the ideas of others. They also alienate everyone around them. Because of this they will lose out in the end.

CHAPTER EIGHT

NOTHING WORKS FOR ME

I'm the eternal optimist and I believe that things will always work out in my favor. This brings its own set of problems and difficulties. In the past I have counted my chickens before they were hatched. I was in a commission business. I would be working on transactions that looked good, and I had every indication that they would end in a deal with a hearty commission check for myself in a month or two. I would count on this in making financial decisions and when the transactions fell apart, I ended up in debt. This is the main reason why I lost my home and family.

I could say it was bad luck or ask why things never work out for me, but I know the truth, it was my actions and my attitude that created my circumstances. I've found that there are many people who think that nothing will work out for them and that they will always end up on the losing side. In everything that they do, they look for the negative and why things will not work, rather than why they will work. If you believe that things will not work, they usually will not.

These kinds of thoughts can also lead to depression. Negativity feeds on negativity. When I was in the depths of my own perfect storm, I was sad and felt sorry for myself. I was drawn to television shows that described the suffering and pain of others. I was drawn to things that showed the problems and pain in society. This did not help anything, it only fed my sorrow and lack of self-worth.

When your own negativity is being fed it is possible to see everything around you as negative. You can believe things are so bad that there is no way things will get any better, and then you portray this attitude to others in the way you speak and act.

When your attitude is negative others will shy away from you and you also may become surrounded by others who are just as negative as you are. If you show this attitude in a job interview you will be passed over for the job and someone more positive will be selected. Your attitude directly affects your ability to succeed.

Always complete what you do and do a bit extra.

So far, I have dealt much with the negative and what not to do. Now I want to deal with the positive. If you say you are going to do something, do it. As scripture says, "let your yes be yes and your no be no." When you do it, do not do it halfway or just enough to get by, do it all the way and a little extra if needed. Sure this may take a bit more of your time and maybe it will not always be appreciated, but in the long run it will be a great benefit to you and others. As I have said, people are always watching and if they see you are there and willing to do what it takes and a bit more, even if it does not benefit you, they will begin to put their trust in you and support you in ways that you may not see or understand.

For example, if you are at the store, don't leave your shopping cart in any parking space, put it in the cart rack or return it inside the store. If you are carrying out the trash and something drops on the ground, pick it up, don't leave it on the ground for someone else to clean up. Go the extra mile at work, do and go where they say. Don't complain or give people a hard time.

Always be upbeat and positive, people do not like complainers. Stand apart from the crowd, being part of the crowd just means you are only as good as the best person and you are as bad as the worst person. Be yourself, be your own person, separate yourself. Be exceptional in all things and never reduce yourself to the lowest common denominator. You are a great person with many talents and abilities, use them. Be confident.

Above all, do not be lazy in life. Trying to get by with doing the least amount of work possible does not work. As my father taught me, do things with gusto, like you mean it. Don't do a half job, or just enough to get by in life. Do what you mean to do with your whole heart, and then move on to your next project. Finish what you start, do a full complete job. Take those extra steps to the garbage rather than dropping your trash and expecting someone else to clean up your mess.

Take ownership of your life and what you do, it is your life and your future, no one else's.

Do your best at all times.

Don't engage in gossip; please do not go to your friends and coworkers talking or complaining about other friends or coworkers. You know the old adage: "if you have nothing good to say…." There are those who go around and all they do is complain and criticize others and their abilities; it is just constant. Often these people are trying to build themselves up by tearing down others. What they do not realize is that it reflects badly on them. Always try to remain positive and upbeat. If you are known as a critic, others will not trust you or believe you. As you know, what people say about others is how they talk to others about you.

Related to this are people who constantly try to build themselves up by talking about how great they are. This gets to be tiring after a while. Both of these attitudes come from a lack of self-confidence. Be kind and understanding to everyone you meet.

Above all, be honest with yourself and others. Deal with facts and reality, not with what you think or hope things should be. If you have problems, do not hide it from those who need to know. As I said, I hid our true financial difficulties from my wife. I should have been open and honest with her all along so we could face and work through those difficulties rather than letting them fester and grow. I messed up, I over extended myself and put our family at risk. I admit this now, but I felt like I could not admit it then. If I would have been open then we could have made changes and not have had to go through the later difficulties.

Show thankfulness. Show your thankfulness to God, show thankfulness to others. As children, our parents taught us to say please and thank you. This does not and should not end when we reach adulthood. People like to be appreciated for their work or assistance that they give. Don't you? Show the same respect to those around you.

What comes to mind here is the teaching of Jesus at the beginning of the Sermon on the Mount, the Beatitudes. Let's take a look at it together:

> *Blessed are the poor in spirit,*
> *for theirs is the kingdom of heaven.*

What does it mean to be poor in spirit? It means not to have the arrogant know it all attitude, thinking that we know more than the next person, so we do not listen to them. That we realize that God is all knowing and all powerful and that he will do what is right and best and that we submit ourselves to the will and guidance of the Lord.

> *Blessed are those who mourn,*
> *for they will be comforted.*

What do we mourn over? We mourn over our own sin and going our own way in life and not seeking the guidance of the Lord. When we realize our own imperfection and lay our cares and concerns upon the Lord we shall be comforted by His grace and blessings.

> *Blessed are the meek, for they will inherit the earth.*

To be meek means to be mild, gentle, and to have humbleness. These attributes will bring you a long way in life and you will gain the respect of those around you.

> *Blessed are those who hunger and thirst for righteousness,*
> *for they will be filled.*

As I said we always need to do what is right and truthful, not just what we think is in our best interest at the time. This means we do what is right and if we strive or hunger for what is right, it will pay dividends in our future. Years ago I read the book The Once and Future King. One of the phrases that struck me and stuck with me is that "Might does not make right," but we use our might for right.

Blessed are the merciful,
for they will be shown mercy.

Show mercy unto others; do not judge them for their weaknesses and mistakes.

Blessed are the pure in heart,
for they will see God.

Be pure in your heart, in your words and deeds, do not lie or mislead others.

Blessed are the peacemakers,
for they will be called children of God.

Do not be one who causes arguments or discourse and unrest. Be peaceful and others will be drawn to you.

Blessed are those who are persecuted because of righteousness,
for theirs is the kingdom of heaven.

If we make the preceding attitudes part of our life and nature, there are those who will not like it and criticize us for it. Do not listen to them, keep the course and blessings will be yours.

CHAPTER NINE

THE BLAME GAME VS. RESPONSIBILITY

It is so important to take responsibility for your own actions if you want change to come into your life. This is not to say that all of the problems you face are your fault, however it matters how you meet every challenge and problem.

When you are going through difficult times it can be easy to blame your problems on other people and what is going on around you. You have thoughts like, "It is not my fault that I do not have a job. The economy is bad. I have problems at work because my boss does not like me. She is spreading lies about me or he is always sabotaging my effort. Everyone is against me and that is why I have these problems." I could go through a whole litany of excuses that I have heard or have said at times, I'm sure you can think of many as well.

As long as you keep placing the blame on others for your problems you will not be able to move forward in your life and take advantage of opportunities that come your way. You could miss out on opportunities that lead to success and prosperity, or at least make your conditions and circumstances better. If you are stuck in the past and place blame on others for your circumstances, you will not find the source of your problems or find out why things are the way they are.

Sometimes people say their problems are because of how they were raised, blaming their parents and how they were treated by others. They place blame everywhere but where it belongs: on them, their actions and attitudes. What happened in the past is past. We are all responsible for our own actions and how we respond to life's situations. We must all come to terms with our past and not let it destroy our future. Don't look back, always look forward.

It is important to look in the direction that you are going in. If you are constantly staring off to the left or the right while driving, that is the direction that you will move. If you are driving and not paying attention and not watching where you are going, you will run off the road and get into an accident. If the car in front of you stops and you are not watching where you are going, you will run into them. It does not work to say it is not your fault that the car stopped, or that you did not see it because you were texting. In a court of law you would be found guilty of distracted driving and receive a huge fine or maybe even end up in jail.

If you are constantly looking elsewhere in life, distracted instead of being focused on where you are going, you can lose your way, go off in the wrong direction, and miss chances to better your situation. You will be subject to danger and have the possibility of getting into an accident and making life worse. If you don't pay attention to your life or to where you are going you are headed for disaster.

Likewise if you are focused on what happened to you in the past that is where you will be living, in the past. You will not be present in your life or ready to move into the future. You will remain in the pain and sorrows that you experienced in the past. You can become tricked by euphoric recall of the past and miss the good times, believing that you had it better then.

The happy memories of the past, will always look better than the trials of the present. This will make you feel that your current situations are worse than they actually are and become negative about the future, believing that things will not improve and will only become worse.

Negativity about the future can almost certainly keep you stuck. When offers or opportunities come where you can improve your situation, you may intentionally miss them. Your fear that things will never be better may keep you from trying. You may begin to look for and find fault in everything and in everyone. This is why you cannot live with your focus elsewhere; you need to live in reality and in the here and now. Take on the challenges of the here and now. The past is the past and cannot ever be changed or relived once it is over. Always move forward.

Take an honest assessment of yourself, who you are and what you want to become. If you want to move forward then self-pity and the past have no place in your life. Successful people do not blame others. Successful people are not stopped by the problems of life. Successful people do not let the past stop them from moving forward into the future. Get rid of that which is holding you back from growing and moving into a brighter, productive and successful future.

Make the changes necessary to move forward, so you can take advantage of the blessings and opportunities that the Lord provides. Recognize that the Lord wants to bless you. His blessings are right in front of you where they always have been. If you look back or to the left or the right and those around you, you may miss it. Look forward so you can move forward. Moving forward requires change, which can be hard, but it is necessary.

As I mentioned in a previous chapter, back in the early 90's I was engaged to a lovely young woman, and because of her doubts the engagement was broke off. I went through a great deal of pain and sorrow because of this and the shadow of this affected other parts of my life for a period thereafter.

Everything that I went through after the day that the engagement was broke off, except for the financial ramifications is fully my responsibility. The problems that I experienced after my divorce and house foreclosure is my sole responsibility, no one else's. This is true no matter how much I try to blame circumstances, others, or the economy. The sooner I realized that the responsibility of my problems, o hardships, and losses, was mine, was the sooner that my life became better.

At times you may need help to get beyond what has taken place in your past. The Lord is there to help you through hard times and the difficulties that can weigh you down. The Lord can arrange things or bring people into your life that can assist you and help you with your healing process. You just need to accept the help and accept the way that the Lord leads. Open your heart to Him and His love and guidance. Say to the Lord, "Your will be done, for I know what You do and provide is for the best for me and my life. I know that You will provide all things necessary for me to continue and to come under Your blessings."

Accept the people that God sends to help you. Learn from them, they are there for you. In some cases He will bring people together to help each other. Every person has their own strengths and weaknesses. Every person has their own knowledge base that has been constructed throughout their lifetime. Sometimes people are brought together to help each other through the lowest points in their lives.

This has recently happened to me. The Lord has brought someone into my life that has helped me considerably with the healing process of all that I have been through and is actually a big reason that I'm now writing this book. I have known Amy for over 40 years and had lost touch with her for most of that time. We met up again at our high school reunion and learned that we have both experienced difficulties. I hope that I was able to help her in some way, as she perhaps unknowingly was able to help me with what I was going through. She has been a light that has shone into the darkness that engulfed my life.

The Lord helps us and assists us, even though we do not realize it or at times we do not want to admit it. We may not always like what we have to live through, but the Lord has a plan and knows what we need and will need in the future.

PART TWO

HOW THE LORD PROVIDES

·

CHAPTER TEN

MONTANA 89

As I briefly mentioned in an earlier chapter, during Christmas of 1989 I took a trip to Montana to visit a young lady that I had met about eight months before. I left on Christmas Day and had planned to spend about four days there. Actually the entire week before I left, I had a bad feeling about going and had considered canceling the whole trip. Maybe this was the Lord trying to tell me something, but I thought that it was nothing and I decided to go anyhow. I did not want to lose the money that I had already paid for the trip. My family was out of town spending Christmas with one of my brothers, so I had Christmas dinner with friends, and they dropped me off at the Chicago O'Hare airport. The young lady picked me up from the airport in Billings, Montana and we left for her house.

Remember that I had a bad feeling before I left, I guess that was warning sign number one. When we left the airport, it was snowy and icy and she lost control of the car and ran off the road. I had to push her out of the snow bank, so this was now warning number two. Everything went well that night as well as the following day and night. I think that we had a good time together - she is really a great person and I did and still do care for her. I will say now that I hold no blame or ill will towards anyone for what was about to happen.

I do know that some of my old friends have made stupid comments and criticisms, but they do not know what they are talking about. They know who they are and if they happen to read this book they should make every effort to apologize to the one that they spoke about.

Now back to the story. On the third day, there were three of us that were going to take a trip from Billings, Montana to Red Lodge at the entrance to Yellowstone National Park. We had a good trip and a good time at Red lodge, played in the snow and such.

On the way back to Billings we were all a bit tired. My one friend fell asleep in the back seat of the car and I was kind of dozing on and off in the passenger seat. The driver woke me up and said to look at the person in the back seat, while still driving and looking back.

Remember what I said about always looking where you are going and not diverting your attention? Here is a prime example of what can happen if you do not pay attention to where you are going, and look at what is behind you.

I will mention that the driver was 16 at the time and an inexperienced driver. While she was looking back the car began going off the road, and at this point, I had the thought, "here we go again." Four days later I woke up in the hospital quoting the bible.

The real story is what took place during the period between the thought, "here we go again," and waking up in the hospital. As we went off the road, the car hit a cross ditch and flipped end over end, landing back on its wheels. Always wear your seat belt. Because I had a seat belt on I was not thrown from and crushed by the car. There was a driver in a car behind us who saw the accident and pulled over to see if we were okay. The girl who was driving had some injuries and the girl in the back seat was pretty much okay, but I was knocked out and actually choking on my tongue. I could not breathe. The Good Samaritan driver saw this and moved the tongue out of my throat so I could once again breath. The Lord had sent someone to save my life.

The ambulance came from Red Lodge, a small town, and they did not have all the necessary life-saving equipment on board. They saw that I was in rough shape so they radioed ahead to the hospital in Billings to send an ambulance to meet them halfway so they could transfer me to a better equipped ambulance.

The ambulance that I was in arrived at the meeting point and I had stopped breathing. They did not have a respirator on board. So here I was not breathing with no way beyond mouth to mouth resuscitation to help me breathe. Even with mouth to mouth, from what I hear after a few minutes there is irreversible brain damage, and the longer the mouth to mouth respirations has to continue, the less of a chance there is for survival.

The good thing is that they did not have to wait that long, because the other ambulance from Billings showed up and they were able to transfer me and hook me up to a respirator. That was the second time the Lord stepped in that day to save my life, or the third, because I was not killed instantly in the accident, which certainly could have happened if I was not wearing my seatbelt.

When I arrived at the hospital they discovered that I had a compound fracture of my left leg, a broken pelvic bone and the big one, a broken neck. It was a C2 fracture. For those who do not know, the C2 is the second vertebrae in your neck, that part of the spine surrounds the brain stem. They call a C2 fracture a hangman's break because it is the vertebrae that breaks when a person is hung. There is part of the C1, or first vertebrae that extends down into the second. If the second vertebrae breaks that part of the first vertebrae goes into the brain stem, it kills you instantly.

Now on top of all this I did suffer brain damage as I had been knocked unconscious during the accident and had some bleeding in the brain. Knowing this, the doctor did not want me waking up with the brain damage and thrashing around with a broken neck, so I was put into a drug induced coma.

Now that you have the background information, we can get to the good stuff, but not quite yet, there are a few more things that you need to learn or understand about me beyond what happened with the accident.

The father of the girl, who I had gone out to visit, and the driver of the car, was a nurse at Deaconess Medical Center where we were hospitalized. He saw the three of us being brought into the hospital. I was in bad shape, to say the least, and his daughter was not in the best of conditions either. In fact all the people who knew my contact information were hospitalized. The only way that they were able to contact my family and tell them what had happened was through our church, the New Apostolic Church. From Montana they contacted the church office who contacted one of my brothers. My parents were out at my other brother's house for Christmas, so the first brother to receive the news called my second brother who drove 45 minutes to where my parents were that evening to tell them in person rather than by phone. He then drove them two hours home that night. My parents flew to Montana the next day and the doctors told them that they did not expect me to live.

My family is part of the New Apostolic Church, which is a worldwide church, led by our Chief Apostle. Under him we have district Apostles that are over countries or regions, then Apostles over smaller territories, Bishops and so on. My father was what we call a district evangelist over a group of congregations. When I was in the accident, my father called our Apostle who contacted our district Apostle. The District Apostle knew who I was, because 6 months before I had stayed at his house one weekend for a church get together in Canada where he lived. He had also been at my home a few weeks before. They said that they would pray for me and the District Apostle told our Chief Apostle who was also praying for me. I was part of the youth organization of the church, and they were praying for me in the area where I lived, around Chicago, plus other parts of the country. Church members from around the country and from different parts of the world were all praying for me. I knew many people and these were the days before internet and social media.

The night before I woke from the coma, the youth group that I belonged to, had a pre-planned get together and they all prayed especially for me. An older member of my church, who had lost her husband, a priest in our church, a few years before, had a dream. In that dream she was in my hospital room and she saw her late husband and another priest who had also passed away a few years prior, standing over my hospital bed. Both these men had been my priests as I was growing up. She asked them what they were doing in my room. They told her that they had come to take me into eternity, but the prayers on earth had stopped them. The next morning I awoke from the coma.

I do have one memory from the time between the accident and the time that I awoke from the coma. It was like a dream and in that dream it was like

I was underwater and could not breathe. I was swimming to a light on the surface and as soon as I reached the light I felt an intense peace. The next thing I knew, I could breathe again. Then I remember waking up with doctors and my parents at my bedside.

This story demonstrates how the Lord works. We may not know or recognize what is going on, but the Lord is always there working for our benefit. He was working on my behalf from April 1989 when I met this girl on a youth weekend and she actually stayed at my home, to the point in August of staying at the home of our District Apostle in Kitchener, Canada, to the events that brought him to my home a few weeks before I left for Montana, to the warnings that I ignored concerning my trip.

All the prayers and the preservation of my life laid the foundation for the following 24 years of my life and the writing of this book. Everything has a purpose and a reason in life, you just have to find out why and what it is. We will explore those topics in the following pages of this book.

CHAPTER ELEVEN

I HAVE TRIED TO DO THINGS RIGHT, WHY DOESN'T THE LORD HELP ME?

Have you asked yourself, "Why doesn't the Lord help me?" The answer is He does, He always offers His help to us. One day during a church outing some of the ministers went on a hike with some of the children. During this hike, one of the kids became sick and two of the ministers took her back to the youth camp. It was hot and tiring but after two hours they made it back. After they arrived, the ministers were thirsty from the arduous walk and they went to the lodge to get something to drink. On their way to the lodge, a flock of seagulls flew over and "let loose," shall we say. One of the ministers got hit in the forehead with a load of seagull poop. This can make one wonder why after doing a good deed, helping a young person arrive safely back where they could receive help, that this minister got hit with such a thing. That is just how things are at times, with no rhyme or reason, they just happen.

Sometimes things happen that aren't so simple and we need help. The problem is that we either do not recognize the help or we don't want to recognize it. At times we reject it because it is not what we think we want. The Lord is always there for us, not only for those who believe in Him but for everyone. As the bible states, the Lord desires all men to be saved. He loves each and every one of us even if we don't always love Him back. He knows what we need and provides it for us. He knows our future, He knows our past. He knows our weaknesses and our strengths. As the bible also states He knew each of us before we were born, He even knew us before the foundation of the earth was laid. He gives us what we need, not necessarily what we want at the time.

As we have discussed, many times it is, us, ourselves, our attitude and actions that create many of our problems. The Lord knows this, He wants to help us, but all too many times our attitude, actions, will and our own ideas, get in the way. We have a free will; we decide what we will do and where we will go. We can choose to follow what He wants or we can choose to follow our own will. We must be ready to face the outcomes that go with each.

I wonder why we question the Lord in his great overwhelming wisdom. He knows and does what is right and good, why should we question His methods? Perhaps it is human nature to question Him. In this way we are like little children questioning their parents. We do not understand, we do not know why, so we question.

We need to look at our lives and see what the Lord has done for us. I know that this can be difficult, sometimes it can feel like our whole life is upside down, one problem after the other. When this happens all we see are difficulties and we can be engulfed in fear. We can become focused on the problems of our lives and not see the good that is all around us. We cannot see the help that has been and is being provided for us. All we see is pain and we feel like we are being smothered by life. When we are focused on the problems we cannot see the blessings of the Lord; we feel that we have been forsaken by God and that his goodness and blessings are being withheld from our lives.

CHAPTER TWELVE

IF YOU WOULD HAVE...

When we feel like we are not being helped by the blessings of the Lord, when our life is in complete turmoil, when we are down and out, we often will try to place blame for our situation elsewhere. When we find someone or something that we can blame for our difficulties we will or can begin to say "If You" would have done something, this would have happened, things would be okay, if you would have done this or helped with that everything would be different, if you, if you, if you.

I have seen this time and time again with my children. They would say if you would have gotten me up earlier for school I would not have missed the bus. What they did not recognize is that I would be in there for 45 minutes before they got out of bed trying to get them up.

My kids, like many today, are big on Video games. When they were younger, when we picked them up from school on Friday, we would take them to the video store to rent a couple of games that they could play over the weekend and we would return them before the store opened on Monday morning. It seemed like a normal routine on Sunday night or Monday morning as we were trying to get the kids up and ready for school, I would end up searching through their rooms for the games or the cases that the games came in.

Let me insert this here, like many young boys, my kids were not the neatest people and their rooms would be a mess. At times I would find the game, but not the case and would return the game, without the case, so I would not receive late fees. Then maybe a week or two later I would find the case. Of course it was my fault or my wife's fault that the game could not be found. At times my boys said "If you" would have told me earlier that I needed to get the games ready then you would not have had to search for them. "If you" would have done this or that, then the games would have been found and you would not have to pay the late fees.

Often times we can be like my kids. We did not or do not get what we want, and we are in difficulties and problems we can say or question the Lord by saying or thinking if you God, would have helped me here or there then I would be in a better situation. If you would bless me with a better Job and more money I would have the money to do more things for you, I could help more people, and I could give more to charity. Then I could take better care of myself and then I could then live in a better situation, have a better house and so on and so on.

Another one is, I'm suffering through many problems and difficulties, and we continually pray to the Lord for help, and we do not see any help or actually things get worse. Then we can say or think, "If you" would help me, things would be better, why don't you help me? Maybe we are going through hard problems, we pray that these problems get taken away, but are not, we can think "If You" would only help me, I thought you loved me why don't you help.

I'm reminded of St Paul here, who shows us the correct attitude when we have to live through difficult times. Paul writes that he had a difficulty that reduced his ability to do the Lords work. He prayed to God that this difficulty to be removed, it was not. Paul did not accuse the Lord for not taking away this illness or difficulty, rather he said that it was the Lords will and that he would accept the burden that they Lord had given him.

When we accuse the Lord for not answering our prayers in the way we want or when we want, we are not only blaming the Lord for our past and current circumstance but also for any future problems that could arise.

When we say "If You" we are removing any personal responsibility for our circumstance and placing them elsewhere. What are we actually saying when we say "If you". We are removing our own responsibility so we are taking the "I" out of the equation and placing the responsibility elsewhere. What do we get with "if you" when we take the I out, we are in fact saying "F You" to God or others, because you did not do this or that or help me here or there. It is worse yet when we say this to God and blame Him for our circumstances, conditions or problems.

We need to learn to take personal responsibility for our circumstances, and then we can begin to grow in our lives. Once we take ownership of our lives by admitting that we are responsible then we can make the changes necessary to change the conditions that we live under.

The Lord wants to bless us and help us, even though we do not always deserve his help and blessings. He will be there for us even though we may say "F You" to him, from time to time. It is up to us to take hold of those blessings, it is up to us to see that we need to change our lives and ways, so we can accept His blessings. The Lord wants us to change to be better people and allows us to go through conditions and circumstances so we can realize that yes we need to change, that we are not the best that we can be. He wants us to take ownership of our faults and failings. Taking ownership of our failings is the first step towards repentance and forgiveness.

We need to take ownership of our lives and or circumstances, and lay our needs for the future in the Lords hands, until then we will live in fear of what is going to happen in our lives. Paul writes to Timothy that "God has not given us the spirit of fear..." if we allow God to lead our life, there is no need to fear. When we put everything in God's hands, He will always do what is best.

Rather than saying "if you" to others when things don't go right in our life and we have problems, say "if I" to them and to yourself. "If I" would have done things differently, "if I" would have done this myself, like I should have, then thing would have worked and everything would be better in my life. Again it comes down to personal responsibility and not pushing your problems off on others in your life

CHAPTER THIRTEEN

I'M SCARED OF WHAT MIGHT HAPPEN TO ME

There is so much we can become fearful of in our lives. We watch the television news or read the papers and we see the dangers in the world today. Of course in the media, many of the problems and dangers that are out there are hyped up to improve their own ratings and sales. If we watch television at all we are inundated by the problems and difficulties of others and the dangers that they face.

I really found this out when I worked nights and after sleeping a bit in the morning would be subject to the wasteland that is daytime TV. All you can find is talk show after talk show highlighting either the problems of others or glorifying media figures. Courtroom television shows are basically the same as the talk shows but in a different format. All they do is highlight the problems and difficulties of others. All in all it is very depressing. Then we have the television news magazines, where they have story after story of how this one disappeared or was killed by their husband, wife, boyfriend or girlfriend, or how one of their kids or other relatives killed or hurt them.

We are surrounded by negativity today; everything highlights the bad in the world today. I have found when watching the local television news that when they cannot find something sensationally bad to say about your local area, they will find something sensationally bad that took place in another state or even in another country so they have something to talk about. Once they find it they talk about it repeatedly.

If we have warm weather or if it gets hot in the summer, then we hear that we have global warming and we better change how we live or we will all burn up. If it is cold in the winter then we have climate change caused by the global warming and we better change the way we live or we will all burn up. Hey wake up it gets hot in the summer and cold in the winter. Sometimes we have warm springs and autumns and sometimes we have cold ones. We have warm winters and cool summers. That is how things work on the planet; climate is always in flux just because it is different than what we think it should be means nothing. There are forces in the solar system and universe that we may not even understand yet that can affect climate. Why do we think that little humans are so great and all powerful that we think that we can control something as massive as the earth's climate? The earth has been hotter and the earth has been colder in the billions of years since its creation, before humans were even on the planet. The earth has been warmer and cooler multiple times in the past few thousand years and guess what we have nothing to do with it. So quite trying to scare us and control us through fear.

This is the problem with the ability to see the news 24 hours a day. They need something to talk about and it makes money for the media if they create some problem so that we will watch the news television specials and movies on the subject. It all comes down to someone making money off of your fear. The problem is that watching this crap all the time will bring you down and can tear you apart.

On the other end you hear over and over about the media darlings, actors and actresses. Their lives are highlighted and you either hear about how their mistakes and problems or about how great they are and how great their lives are. We hear how much better they have it than we do. They are promoted as modern day idols; we even call them that, in fact they are no different than us and are really nothing special. They make their money by pretending that they are someone else. They make their money by having people look at them. The more that they can get their name in the news the better off they are, the more money they can make. This can also bring someone down, if you see how great others have it and compare it to your own life.

There have been many times that I have awakened in the morning fearful of the future and of how I'm going to pay my bills. As I said before, we need to pry this worry and fear from our minds, and we need to give it to the Lord. He will take care of things, we may not like how things are taken care of but they will be taken care of. Remember in many cases we have caused our own problems and this often means we will have to suffer the consequences of our actions.

We cannot expect to look to the Lord and have Him wave his hand and say "All your problems are solved, I'm going to make it so you win $50,000,000.00 in the lottery so all your bills can be paid and all the problems that you got yourself into will be solved." We need to repent of where we have been irresponsible, change our ways and give the problems to the Lord. He will open avenues for our success in taking care of our difficulties but if we are just focused on our problems we will not see those opportunities.

If we are focused on our problems we become negative, about everything, when we become negative about everything we do nothing.

CHAPTER FOURTEEN

WHAT IF?

"What if" is a question you ask when you are analyzing your plans and looking for potential dangers and pitfalls. This question can stop you in our tracks causing a stagnation of development and growth. This question can stop you from changing and moving to a better future and choices. When you ask this question with fear of the future it can prevent you from making any kind of firm decisions.

I have been stopped by the "what if" question many times, "What if I make the wrong choice?" It seems like more often than not I made the wrong decisions in my life. You know my story now, what do you think?

Even after my divorce I refrained from dating. "What if" I got involved in a relationship and my ex decided that she made a mistake and wanted to get back together? What would I do? Of course this was a matter of not wanting to let go of the past and I was constantly looking back and avoiding or missing any chance for a new relationship. Of course there was not even the remotest of possibilities that this would happen, but still, the "what if" question haunted me.

The "what if" question and its problems and dangers became larger in my mind as slowly my life fell apart around me. At times I would be fully paralyzed from making any kind of decision because I would be afraid of making the wrong one and being financially hurt in the process. I had no confidence in myself or ability to make the right choice. This of course hurt me in more ways that you can imagine. The fact that I was unwilling to make choices because of the danger of a financial loss cost me more money than if I just would have made a choice.

Does this sound like you at times? I think we all have a fear of being wrong. It comes from the idea that if you make the wrong choice and others see it you will come under ridicule from your friends and family. It is like walking on ice and slipping. Sure at first they will ask if you are alright, but then the kidding begins. Perhaps men deal with this more harshly, for we are not supposed to make mistakes, slip or screw things up.

Back in the late 80's the company that I worked for purchased a new computer, a top of the line desktop computer with all the bells and whistles that one can think of. We were told by the salesmen that this computer was so advanced that it would be good for the next 10 – 15 years. Well a few years after that, the internet became accessible and technology grew and changed to the point where the computer quickly became obsolete and on the side gathering dust. We had new, faster, cheaper computers with many more capabilities and the old one was trashed.

Should we have purchased the old one, yes we made money with it so it was a good purchase, but if we would have kept it and not purchased new ones for fear that they would also become obsolete, the world and economy would have advanced and changed around us and we would have been left in the dust with an out of date computer that only ran Dos while everyone else was running Windows.

Who wants you to remain in fear? Who wants you to question yourself to the point that you are stagnant in your growth or development? Who places fear of the future in your heart? Is it not the devil? He wants you to be fearful; he despises humans and the abilities that the Lord God has placed in you. He would like nothing more than for you to fall back and cause your own personal destruction. Then he can go to God and say "See, look at your creation that you gave so much to, look what they are doing, they wasted all that You gave them. All Your hope and work is for naught."

The Lord says, "Fear not." If you trust and have faith in the Lord God, He will help you and lead you in the right direction. Yes, He has given you free will and you will make mistakes at times. He will allow this to happen so you can learn and grow. He will always provide for you if focus your faith and love on Him. You may feel like you are sinking at times with no way out, but He will provide for you and open the right paths that you need to follow to return to safety and blessing.

When the paths to safety and blessing open before us you need to see and follow them and not be fearful of what may happen if you do, the Lord has your back, He will always provide and lead you the right way. Don't let the "what if" that the devil whispers in our ear stop us from following that path. The Lord will provide a way out at just the right time. You may sink but He will not let you drown in the troubles of life. He will show you the way and send the right people into your life at just the right time. If we follow His ways, His abundant blessings will overflow upon us.

The Lord is there to lead and guide you. Sometimes you know what you should do but doubt creates an internal struggle. This is what happened to me when I purchased our last house. My heart was telling me "No, do not do it. This is a bad decision. You cannot afford it. "What if" the economy goes down and your income drops, what are you going to do?"

I did not listen to the "What if" question, which was actually serving me well in that instance.

I knew that if I went forward and purchased the house and we lost it, my wife would divorce me, but I did it anyway. There were even signs that the Lord gave me not to move forward with the house. I went into a financial slump and I had a rough road of problems. Actually my income qualified me for the loan, but my credit did not. So the mortgage broker used some creative financing to get the loan approved, as was common in that time. I didn't heed any of the warning signs because I felt like I knew better and that things would work out in the end. Boy was I wrong.

This is similar to the time the Lord tried to warn me before I went to Montana, did I listen? Nope. Did I learn? No. The Lord also warned me about my first engagement a month before we broke up, before we had begun to spend money on our wedding and future together. I felt that something was wrong and I needed to slow things down, but again I did not listen.

When I was in my twenties I had a friend named David. He was a great person. We knew each other from church and we even worked at the same place for a while, though for different companies. I was a painter at the time, and he worked for a carpet cleaning service. He eventually moved away and we lost touch. Years later he came down with a terminal illness which he survived for a few years.

The time came that I was thinking of him many times throughout the day, he was on my mind and in my prayers a lot. Then one Sunday morning a friend told me as I entered church that David had passed away. My first thought was, "I know." No one had told me before that time, but I knew in my heart that he was gone. The Lord had already told me.

The Lord speaks, you just need to listen and follow His ways. He will take you by the hand and lead you to where you need to be and see you through the storms of life.

CHAPTER SIXTEEN

THE LORD'S GPS

It seems like everyone knows a shortcut. I have taken them and I'm sure that you have as well. You know the ones where you take the main four lane highways or even two lane highways to your destination until someone says that they have this great shortcut. They direct you down a side road, then another, and then another. You may miss a stop light and even go fewer miles but you are going at a much slower rate of speed than you would on the main road. Do you save time? It seems so, but I have found usually not so much. People act like you will get to your destination an hour sooner if you take this short cut, when in fact it is only a few minutes or seconds, if that.

One of the neighborhoods we lived in we had this problem. Every morning and every evening there would be car after car going down our narrow residential street, all these people believing that they were going to save a whole bunch of time going down this side road rather than taking the four lane road that was less than a quarter mile north. The only thing they missed was a stop light where they would be making a right hand turn. Instead, with this so-called short cut they had three stop signs and a much slower speed limit, although many did not obey, making it a rather dangerous road with all these cars speeding to their destinations.

Now I'm sure these people believed that they were going to save all this time, but they did not. I actually checked it out one day; I drove both ways and timed myself. I found out that it actually took them more time to go the so called short-cut than if they had taken the main road.

As you can see, short-cuts are not always really short-cuts. You can find this in other areas of life as well. You can take the advised route to achieve success, earn a living, gain wealth, provide for your family, buy a nice home, or whatever you seek. Then there are the short cuts, or what you think are shortcuts to gain those things. More often than not what you think is a short cut to what you want is no more than a dead end or at the least a roundabout route to nowhere. These short cuts can take more time and you can get lost in the process.

I was one that would always try to find a short cut to success. When I had my business I would see what I viewed as a potential short cut and I thought myself so smart that I saw this short cut where no one else did. To many times in the end it was no short cut. This can be seen by looking where I ended up with no home, away from my family and no business.

In many things I smugly thought of myself as so much smarter than the next person that I could take short cuts to success, in financing my home or in whatever it may be. I was always looking for a shorter, quicker route to what I wanted. That is another reason why everything came crashing down in my life. Do you remember the saying, "Speed kills?" Do things right, do not shortcut your success

Many people today use GPS to guide them were they want to go. A few years back we had a GPS that we mostly used in areas where we were unfamiliar, which is the common usage. Sometimes I used it in familiar areas, just to find out if the GPS directions were any different than the route that I would usually take.

With the GPS, if we made a wrong turn or went a different route, the voice on the GPS would say "recalculating, recalculating," and then tell us the way to get back on the prescribed route that it wanted us to go. Every time turned differently than what it said, or passed the road that it wanted us to take, we would hear "recalculating, recalculating." This became a joke to my young kids and we all had a laugh about the constant "recalculating, recalculating."

The Lord can be like our GPS through life. There is a prescribed route that He directs us to follow, being human, we do not always follow the route that He wants us to travel upon. We see and take what we believe as shortcuts, we lose our way, miss turns and the path that the Lord wants us to take. He then recalculates the route that we need to take so we can get back on the right path.

When we go off the prescribed path, that is when we run into trouble, we end up with problems and difficulties. The thing is that we can be stubborn and do not want to change or follow the way back to the Lords path. Then He again recalculates and gives us a new way back to the narrow way that leads to his salvation.

Just like when you are driving and the GPS recalculates the path to the destination and directs you back to the main road, it can take you down streets and alleyways, to get you on the correct route as quickly as possible. Some of these streets can be old, with pot holes and maybe in not so nice areas. The Lord directs us back to His way, and we may have to go down streets and alleyways that are not so nice and our problems and difficulties may seem to increase as we go down these paths back to the correct way, His way. We may have to go through not nice areas with holes that we need to navigate around. Once we are back on His path things get better and we learn and grow as spiritual beings.

What we need to realize is that the Lord has not put us on these roads, alleyways and paths to harm us. The reason why we have to travel down these ways that can be filled with dangers and obstacles is not because of the Lord's choice but ours. We decided to go our own way, to divert from the Lord's way and go our own way. The Lord knows and sees ahead and wants us to avoid greater dangers and problems.

The interesting thing is how quickly and how far off we can be once we miss or make a wrong turn and go in direction that is contrary to the Lords way. In some areas they have streets that run North, South, and East and West that are basically straight. In some places, beside the straight streets they also have angled ones mixed into the network. I know that in some areas, while I was driving, I have gone the wrong direction, missed a turn or taken the wrong way, and it was amazing how far off the right road I had gone in a very short distance. Even after a minute or two, after I had realized that I missed a turn and tried to get back on the right road, I would turn around or take another road that I believed would get me on the right road once again, but it took me twice as long to get back to the right road as what I traveled on the wrong road.

At times in life you go down many side roads that takes you in different directions, left right and left again, and sometimes we have to backtrack just so we can get back to where we were or on the right path once again. The same thing happens when we follow the Lords way. If we go off, even a little, before long we will be so far off of the Lords way, we will be lost and wandering in the darkness that is in the world today.

If you are in one path and your companion is on another, for a while you can walk next to each other. If one path angles even an inch in a different direction than the other, after even a short time you and your companion will end up miles apart. These two paths looked parallel, but in fact were not. If you are in darkness or in an area where you do not have a clear sight of each other, you will not even realize that you have traveled miles apart until you reach your destination and your companion is not there when you arrive. Both of you leave walking together from New York City and you arrive in Vancouver, Canada but your companion arrived in San Diego, California. You may have walked for miles next to one another, but somewhere along the way you separated and did not realize the mistake that was made.

At times we do not understand the way a GPS wants to take us. We know a different way that may be faster than what the GPS is telling us to do. Especially now, the GPS can show you where there is road construction or an accident that would delay your journey. It will try to route you around those hazards. When this happens it may seem like you are going out of your way, but because you do not know the hazards ahead, you do not know the reasons why it is directing you in such a way.

It is the same with the Lord. He knows and sees the hazards in our path that could pose a danger to us or delay us on our journey to his kingdom. He then tries to direct us around those problems and hazards. Like with the GPS, we do not understand why, so we question and may want to take a different way. We need to follow and trust in the Lord and the direction that He wants to lead us.

The Lord knows everything about us, about our future, our past, our faults, our failings, our virtues and all of our abilities. He knows all the mistakes we can, do or will make. He tries to help and guide us through the minefield of our life.

The question is, the Lord knows our future, can we change it?

CHAPTER SEVENTEEN

HAUNTED BY PAST MISTAKES

We all make mistakes in our life, some big some small. I know that I have made some. We can hurt people unintentionally, either physically or emotionally. None of us are perfect and it seems like we thrive at times in our imperfections.

Many of the mistakes I've made have haunted me for days, weeks, months or even years. Even little mistakes have haunted me and nagged at my subconscious. Quite a few years ago, I was driving home from somewhere and a friend was following me. I was going over the speed limit for a while, then I slowed down. Well my friend did not slow down and there was a traffic cop ahead looking for speeders. Well, I believe you can guess what happened; my friend was pulled over for speeding. I had the idea that it was my kind of my fault because I was speeding to begin with. Now every time I drive that stretch of road I think about my friend receiving that ticket and it nags at me.

There are other times in my life that I did things that I'm not proud of, where I made mistakes and said or did the wrong things. Every so often, something reminds me of those situations and it bothers me.   Like one time, when I was 15 years old, I was with a friend and we were going into a parking garage. He had a nice car, only a few months old, that he was very proud of. On his car he had a big antenna that was held onto the roof by a magnet. As we entered the parking garage the antenna began to scrape on the roof of the garage, so he asked me to get out and take the antenna off the car. Well, me being a kid, I got out and rather than tilting the antenna to break the connection to the roof of the car I pulled it to the side until the connection was broke and I brought the antenna into the car.

Of course I shouldn't have done it like that, because as I pulled the antenna I put some deep scratches into the roof of his nice new car. My friend, as you could imagine, was not too happy with me once he saw the damage. I was embarrassed and not too happy with myself either.

He got the damage fixed a short time later and he was aggravated with me for a while but besides that there were no long term effects. Although this was at least 35 years ago, it still bothers me from time to time to this day. He has moved away from the area and I have not seen him in years. The car is a long time in the junk heap, but every so often I think about it and kick myself for this innocent mistake.

Maybe I'm just strange in this way. Does your past bother you? I know that these are innocent examples but for some reason they bother me. You can be bothered by little things or big things but as long as it bothers you, it will affect you. The important thing is to learn from your mistakes, grow to the future and not continually look back and let your past mistakes bring you down.

At times it seems easy to remember the mistakes and the bad times while the good that I may have done gets shoved into the recesses of my brain. The past just nags and brings you down. Even if you do not always think about it, it is always lurking in the back of your mind, bringing you down, making you feel like you are bad, wrong and giving you a low self-worth because of what you may have done. We need to learn to forgive ourselves as we forgive others.

Sometimes other people remind you of what you have done wrong. You can get into an argument with someone or have a discussion and every mistake that you've made or wrong that you've done, or even things that did not affect them directly is brought up. Things that could have happened years or decades before are brought up and you are pounded over the head with them just like it happened yesterday. This often happens because the wrong has not healed in their heart. Maybe what you did was so egregious or hurt them so bad that it is hard for them to heal. Every time that you do something else that hurts them, all the memories of the hurts that they suffered in the past come to the forefront and it is like you ripped off the scab or ripped open a wound that wasn't completely healed. At this point they are in great emotional pain and they may lash out to hurt you like you have hurt them.

This is one thing that husbands complain about with their wives in an argument, I know that I experienced this many times. You and your wife get into an argument and before you know it the wife is giving a rendition of every mistake that you made. I know this is mind boggling to men, it was to me. I could not fathom how my wife could remember things that were said and done over ten years before. Too often I would dismiss this, because to me it was not relevant to the discussion at hand. I wanted to deal with that, not with what happened ten years ago.

What I did not realize at the time, was that the argument was not really about the current problem, but it was really about what happened so many years before. I had done something to hurt my wife and that wound was still in her heart because I had not done anything to help it heal. To me it was not important.

Though we want to, we cannot blame them for their actions here. They are in pain and for one reason or the other the pain is still there and we keep aggravating the wound if we don't change the behavior that caused it to begin with. It would help to treat those we've hurt with love and kindness. Give them time to heal, show love, and respect. If we do not show love and respect it can make matters worse and the hurt and pain will never heal. Instead it will just grow and fester until it poisons friendships or in worst cases relationships and marriage.

Ultimately, the overriding force that keeps bringing up your past and stands in the way of your healing is the devil, Satan, the evil one. He is the one who wants to bring you down, who wants to destroy you and make you think less of yourself. He does not like that the Lord God made you in His image with power and authority, and the devil wants to bring you down in any way that he can. He will pound on you and make you remember your past wrongdoings and tell you that you are not worth anything. He will make the smallest of transgressions seem great.

The Lord, on the other hand is gracious and loving. Through the sacrifice of the Lord Jesus, He provided a way for you to come under His grace and forgiveness. He said that once forgiven sin will be remembered no more. All the Lord asks is that you repent and forgive others just as He has forgiven you. It is so nice easy and simple. Repent and forgive. It is the devil that makes this hard, or makes you think that it is hard, because he always is bringing it up. Tell the devil that you are a child of God and the Lord God has forgiven your sins and they will not be remembered. If your sins, errors, or mistakes have been washed away and forgotten by the Lord, why keep them in your own memory? If the Lord God does not hold your past against you why should you?

CHAPTER EIGHTEEN

BEING JUDGMENTAL

We all know people who are judgmental; maybe we are or have been in the past. We can be held in judgment because of the things that we are currently doing or what we may have done in the past. None of us can be the judge or jury over the actions or inactions of others. Now hear I'm not talking about the natural laws of our country, but Godly laws, or infractions and activities where the laws of humans have not been broken. We see people every day doing or saying things that we feel are not right or in the extreme, not Godly. When this is detected, we can become a judge over others without knowing any background or reasons why. We may not even know the people or what lies in their heart. We do not know reasons why they may be doing what they do or have done. We just see and at times hold them in condemnation.

Things may be simpler than this, maybe we do not like the music that they listen to or that they are playing and we make a quick decision about what kind of person they are. We do not like what they wear, or piercings and tattoos. All of these play a role in how we view people. Yes at times we can feel danger by the way one looks or what they do, this is fine, but to judge them and condemn then is not right.

None of us know what each one has lived through, their pain, sorrow or difficulties. I have learned over the years that people are who they are, we need to accept, we may not always like, but accept who they are.

I have grown to understand, over the years, that people are people, each one with their own problems, difficulties and strange ways. Each one of us are different, are special and have something to add to this life.

I was on a job once where we had to work nights. This was in the south loop in Chicago, or on the southern side of the downtown area. On breaks or lunches we would go outside for a while or take a walk to some 24 hour establishment to get something to eat or drink. At 2:00 AM the roads are empty all you find are the homeless walking the streets looking for something to eat or for money. It is all too easy to brush them off or give them some change and keep going. A few times we just stopped and spoke with them, let them tell us their situations and problems. There was one in particular that was quite interesting. We met him one night while on our lunch; he was homeless and actually did not ask for anything. He just wanted to talk to us and tell us his story and his problems. He needed an outlet and we were there for him. This was one of best nights that I had while I was working down there. It actually started to lay the foundation to begin my writing career. If I would have turned my back on him because of the way he looked or acted, I would have missed a great deal and may not be doing this right now.

The Lord has accepted us, just the way we are. He knows and sees our heart, what lives deep inside, not what is on the exterior. The Lord Jesus spoke about this many times. The life of the Lord is an example of not being judgmental. Many did not like or accept him because of what He did or the people that He associated with. Yes they loved the many miracles that he did, they liked what he said, but they could not accept that he ate and drank with sinners, with prostitutes, and publicans. They judged Him, because they did not like who he associated with. Those that judged Him believed that those he associated with were inferior and that because Jesus associated with them, he was also inferior.

Too many people today worry too much about what other people are doing. They tell us, and can be quite adamant, that we should do this and that we should not to that. The Lord Jesus spoke of this when he spoke about those who worry about the sliver in other people's eyes but do not see the beam in their own eye.

Some today go on crusades to rid people of everything that they feel is wrong or bad for them. These people become obsessed with what others are doing. They complain that people are eating the wrong food, doing the wrong things, thinking the wrong way. Why, because it is different than what they would do or want to do. Did you ever think that they would really want to do it, but do not allow themselves to, so they want to rid the world of any temptation to do it? Or that they are secretly jealous of people who do and want to stop them.

I guess a good example of this is cigarette smoking, we all know that it is bad for you, but many do it. Sure you can have a concern about the health of others, but there are some who take this to a higher level. They go on crusades to end it by everyone to stamp out any desire by anyone to do it. I like to call them anti-smoking Nazis. You could apply this example to any number of things today, it seems like no matter what we do or say there is a group out there trying to end or stop people from doing it.

For myself, I used to be one of those people, going out on a crusade to end all evil in the world, but I have grown to understand that it is just not worth it. I feel that I have too many of my own problems, I need to correct that which I find wrong with myself, and I do not have the time or energy to correct in others what I believe is wrong.

I have learned that we need to accept others, as they are, just as the Lord has accepted us. We cannot try to inflate ourselves by bringing others down. Be positive, be loving, and gracious to others just as God wants to do for you and me.

We need to clean our own house first, before we go and try to clean the house of others. None of us are perfect and have a huge host of issues we need to deal with for ourselves before we can correct the problems in others. The thing is we become so consumed with the problems of others we do not see the problems within ourselves.

Maybe that is the reason why we go on such crusades; we really just do not want to see the problems within ourselves and do not want to deal with them, so we spend our time and energy trying to fix others. We are just trying to avoid working on ourselves; we are trying to avoid changing. We just do not want to recognize that yes we are not perfect, we have problems and we just do not want to deal with them.

We need to deal with our own problems and deficiencies first before we go out and work on the problems and deficiencies of others.

This goes into what I mentioned before, that we need to keep focus on ourselves and not look at others or look in other directions. Fix yourself first, pay attention to yourself and your problems and look for ways to grow and improve yourself, before you spend the time and energy trying to improve others.

The Lord gave each one a free will to decide for their own life as they see fit. He trusted in us that much, He knew that some would fail and fall, but he also knew that some would grow into his likeness and attain salvation. He left it in our hands, he can and does try to guide us, but the ultimate decision on what path and road we take is all up to us.

Who are we to become little gods and try to dictate what others do or what they say? It is called freedom. Freedom of choice of decisions of what they do with their life with no one standing over them and telling them how wrong they are and that they cannot do this or that. As long as what you do does not negatively affect the freedoms of others there is no person or government that can dictate to you what you do, say, eat, drink or anything. To many want to control others, this is wrong. When they try to control others they show how judgmental that they are, and this is ungodly. Unless you repent and change your ways it will keep you out of, and away from the salvation that was offered by the Lord Jesus.

Each one of us has been granted the love and grace of God. He does not judge us for our mistakes and sins. Rather He sent Jesus, who gave His life on the cross so our sins could be forgiven. Sin does not matter, focusing on sin will not lead you to salvation. Focusing on sin will only make you judgmental of yourself and of others. Rather our focus should be directed according to the teaching of Jesus that was love, the overwhelming love for God and the Love for those around us.

CHAPTER NINETEEN

I'M STUCK, WHAT DO I DO?

At times we feel trapped, we live in a bad situation, we do not know what to do or where to go. What do we do? We can pray to God and ask him to change it, but then what. We cannot just sit around waiting for a huge flash and everything will be okay. At times we do not know what to do, what path to take. Do we wait or go our own way. What is the right thing to do?

I have struggled with this question many times; I still struggle with this, what is the right thing to do.

We can hear the phrase that the Lord helps those that help themselves. Is this the right thing, I'm not sure, in a way yes and in a way no. In one context of that saying we are putting our faith and trust into what we can do, as a human to better our circumstances, we are deciding. This fits with the idea that the Lord gave us a free will to decide for ourselves. With this though we are also imperfect and do make the wrong choices and decisions when we only trust in our own abilities. We need to put our trust and accept the help and guidance of the Lord and not trust in ourselves. When we trust in ourselves we will go the wrong way and make the wrong choices.

Yes, the Lord gave us a free will to make choices for ourselves, which is the one thing that we have that is completely ours. What is the one thing that we can truly give him, that is fully meaningful, is it not our own free will. This will show that we love and trust the Lord to lead and guide us in the right paths or ways.

This still does not answer the question, what do we do? Do we sit back and lay it in the Lords hands, trusting in him, in a way yes, in a way not so much. If we do not like the situation that we are in we need to change it. If you cannot win the unwinnable game, you change the rules. We need to do what we believe is right based on the information at hand. We can pray and ask the Lord for his guidance, but once that guidance is there we accept it and follow it. We cannot ask for his help and guidance and then go our own way.

I have done this, prayed for his guidance and then went my own way; it does not turn out good.

I actually did this when I was considering purchasing my last house. I asked Him for His guidance if I should purchase it or not. He told me no, did I listen, you know that answer by now.

If we ask for his help we need to follow the help and guidance. If receive His help and guidance, and then still go our own way based on what we want and not what the Lord wants, we are rejecting the Lord and it would have been better for us if we had never asked to begin with. Our problems that we need to have our eyes open so we can recognize the help when offered.

This goes back to looking at where we are going and not in any other direction. There are times where we can become so focused on what we want and we miss what the Lord wants for us. We miss the road to a better outcome than what we had in our own mind. We are looking away from the Lord and looking within ourselves.

In the bible, when Moses was leading the children of Israel through the Sinai desert from Egypt to the Promised Land, at one time the Lord allowed poisonous snakes to go into the camp. This was to test the people and see their faith in the Lord. The Lord had instructed Moses to have the people look up and not look down and he would make sure that they would be safe.

Now, this is contrary to what we or what many of them thought was best and the safest way at the time. They were to look up and not watch out for the dangers on the ground all around them, does not sound logical or right. As it turned out all of those who followed the instruction of the Lord were saved and those that did not look up and looked down to what was around them were bit by the snakes. Those that were bitten trusted in themselves and what they saw was safe and right, the others who were saved trusted in the Lord, his vision and followed the way that He knew was best.

I'm sure that many of you have heard this story before, but I will use it for an example.

A man was in his house and a knock came at the door, he answered the door and there was a person there that warned him that he better leave the house because a flood was coming. The man in the house said no worries the Lord will provide.

Well the water began to rise and the man's house was surrounded by water and the water was creeping up the walls. Some people came in a boat and said the waters rising, come get into the boat and we will take you to safety. The man said again, I'm fine I know my Lord will provide for me and I will be okay.

Well the water kept on rising and before long the man was on the roof of his house, a helicopter came and they yelled down, come grab the ladder and climb into the helicopter we will save you, come get in now or you will drown.

The man once again said no, I have faith in God and I know that he will help and protect me from this flood. You can go now I'm fine and please do not bother me anymore.

Well the waters kept on rising and the man drowned. When he got to heaven he asked the Lord, I prayed and had faith that you would help me, why did you let me drown.

The Lord said that I tried to help you three times, I warned you and tried to give you a way to save your life, but you said no.

He did not accept the help that was offered by the Lord, he had his own ideas of what he believed the Lords help would be. He had faith in God, he prayed to God, he asked for help, but when God sent help he said no to God and he ended up suffering the consequences. He thought that God would just save him, maybe with a big flash and poof the flood would be gone, or the water would divide like the red see around his home and he would be safe. He did not see God in those that he had sent to save him from the waters.

After the children of Israel left Egypt and were entering the Promised Land, they came upon the city of Jericho. This was a great walled city that stood in their way between the desert behind them and the Promised Land which stood before them. The Israelites sent two spies into the city to do what spies to best be secretive and gather information.

These spies were in a strange land, a strange city and the rulers of that city knew that the Israelites were coming and knew their intentions. Often times spies need someone, especially in this case that can work on the inside, someone who can help them and protect them. Who helped them? Was it some great person? Someone who was a good or as some would say today the right kind of person? No it was not, it was a harlot who helped then, someone who some would consider on one of the lower rungs of society.

If the spies would have said to themselves this in not the right kind of person who should help us, surely the Lord would send us someone else, someone that fits our standards, not a lowly harlot that sells her body for money? We will wait for someone that we will approve of, not this person.

If they had done this, what would have happened? They would have been stuck in that city and maybe even captured or killed, and who knows, maybe the Children of Israel never would have taken the Promised Land and the whole history of the world would be different.

Do we accept the guidance of the Lord; do we accept those that he has sent to lead us through this time? Or do we say those are not the "right kind" of people, and dismiss the help that they can give. We cannot be the judge of whom or what the Lord works through or gives his message through, Remember he even used a Mule or an Ass to speak though and to give his message.

So now back to the initial question, what do we do, how we proceed. We do what we need to do, proceed in a direction that we feel in our heart is right. Keep our ears and eyes open to the worlds and guidance of the Lord. We know in our heart of hearts what to do and we proceed in that direction until shown otherwise. We pray and ask for help and guidance, and accept that which is given. Listen, it may not, most likely will not be in a big flash or epiphany, it will be simple and quiet, a whisper. He will say to us that we should do this or that or go that way or this way. We can and will see warning signs of going the wrong way, just listen to them.

Like before I went to Montana in '89 and ended up in the hospital, I had a warning, but decided to proceed anyhow. I actually had two warnings, but still proceeded. We may not always choose the right way or listen when the warning signs are there, but we learn and grow from the mistakes that we make, or at least we are supposed to. At times we need to go through the same type of problems over and over, or at least it seems that way until we learn and grow.

CHAPTER TWENTY

WHY DO BAD THINGS HAPPEN WHEN THINGS ARE GOING WELL?

I have often wondered why bad things suddenly happened when everything was going well in my life. It also seemed that once the bad started it would go on and on. Did I do something wrong? Was the Lord punishing me for something?

Let's get this clear, the Lord will not hurt or punish you because of mistakes we make today. Yes, in the days of the Old Testament, He did punish many for their sins during their lifetime. We do not live in that time period. We live under grace. The Lord Jesus was sent and died for our sins and the grace of God comes upon us. He can and will forgive us for our actions, if we repent and seek His grace. If not then we will come under His judgment, not during our lifetime but at the end of time when all souls will be judged.

Remember what I said before, we often make choices and decisions that take us off the path that the Lord has set before us and we end up on a different path that has many pitfalls. This is not because the Lord is punishing us in any way, but we are now on a path of our own choosing and the difficulties are because of the choices that we make, by our own free will. They are not a punishment from the Lord. I spent the whole first section of this book showing how the choices that we make hurt us; it is not the Lord putting obstacles in our way. The Lord loves each one of us and only wants the best for us.

Now, if we are not being punished for our sins or indiscretions and if we have not done anything that we can think of that has put us on a different path than the one the Lord has set before us, why then, at times, do bad things happen to us after times of good and prosperity? It is not a punishment, but look at it this way; it is out of Love and the blessing of the Lord God.

Okay, I hear you, how could these bad things, this bad situation that I'm in or going through be out of love or a blessing? If this is a blessing what are we doing? I thought that God was a loving God who only wants the best for us.

He does only want the best for us. We may not understand it, or like that we have to face difficulties and problems. So how are the difficult circumstances that we have to live through be considered a blessing? As mentioned before, the Lord knows our future; he knows what we are going to have to face in our life. He knows our future, what will happen to us.

I noticed in my life, especially while being short on finances, that I would earn more money and get a little savings in the bank, finally think that I was getting ahead, but then something would happen and before I knew it I had to spend all the money. I wondered why, things were going so well, why did they stop?

A few months back I was on the highway and was hit by a semi-truck. He kept going and I could not get a license number or company name from the truck. My car was damaged but still drivable. I filed a claim with my insurance and they decided that the cost of repair was greater than what the car was worth, so they totaled out the car and gave me a check for the value of my car. I was able to keep the car.

My plans were to use the money to purchase a new vehicle, but as things worked I could not get approved for financing. So I decided to just bank the money for a while and save the car payments until I would have a very large amount to put down. This seemed like a good plan. Well, as things went, about a month after the accident, my income decreased by just over $200.00

per month. Living with limited resources and expenses that continue with a decrease of that amount is huge. With that decrease I would have been unable to make any kind of car payments and would have ended up with my car being repossessed by now; good thing that I did not buy a new car.

Now as stated I have some big expense obligations, so that money came in handy to help cover my expenses for a couple of months. It was a benefit that I had that money. I was able to use it for what I needed since my income had been reduced.

Now we can look at the accident as a bad thing, but no one was hurt. My car is fine except for a few dents and a duct-taped window. It was not the best that I could not find out who hit me, so I could not get a huge settlement from the trucking companies' insurance, but that was not the Lord's intention.

It would have been nice to have a new car rather than one with 200,000 miles on it, but the Lord had other plans. He knew that other problems would be coming my way including my reduction in income and He blessed me in such a way that I would be able to make it through and still be able to pay my expenses and most of all my child support. This was not only a blessing for me, but also for my ex-wife and my kids.

Looking back on this situation, I was also warned that this would happen. A few months prior I started having the thought that I was going to be hit by a truck. I do not know why, it just came to me. I knew it and I was being warned of this event.

We need to realize and come to terms with the fact it is not always just about us, but what we do, go and say has ramifications beyond us and even our immediate family. Our lives are like a huge jigsaw puzzle we are all pieces in a huge picture. We are all interconnected, we live though and experience things that may give us a personal benefit or not, some things that we live through or experience are for the benefit of others, someone we may not even know.

Our lives are interconnected, each of our choices have an effect on another or a number of other people on the earth. We need to grow and realize that everything is just not about us. What we want or for our own self comfort. We cannot be so inner focused that we believe that we are the only ones that matter. Everyone is equal, has the same rights as we. Be considerate of others and their needs. As the golden rule states, "do unto others as you would have them do unto you".

What I have lived through or write in this book may serve to help you or another or a great number of people. We just do not know. The only one that knows is the Lord God, he has a good reason for all, and so we accept and deal with what happens to us the best that we can. We know that all is for the best; we will explore this subject in the next section of this book. We will look at the theory of predestination and if we can change our future. What if we would have gone left rather than right, if we would have taken another job, married another spouse or whatever we can think of. Life is full of options and choices, some with greater ramifications than others.

PART THREE

THE LORD DOES WHAT IS RIGHT FOR US

CHAPTER TWENTY-ONE

I JUST WANT TO GET MY LIFE BACK

When you are in a place where you feel you do not belong, when you have been beaten down with problem after problem, after you have lost everything and you are in a place that you do not like, you may have thoughts of

"Where am I?
Why am I here?
I just want to get my life back.
I do not belong here."

You don't know why you had had to go through it or why you have setback after setback, problem after problem. The problems that you live through can be constant, every day, every week, month after month and even year after year. You may have been beaten down but you take one step forward and things look like they are improving only for you to get knocked down again. You want nothing more than a normal life, a home, family, and at least enough to get by.

You are tired of lying in bed awake night after night, wondering what you are going to do. How are you going to feed your family, keep your house? If you do get to sleep, you wake up in the middle of the night with a sense of deep fear and intense worry about the next day and what it will bring. Just when you think that you have reached the bottom, it all falls out and you are in a freefall once again.

It gets to the point where you just do not know what to do, you are done, and you cannot do it anymore. One cannot make clear choices or decisions. Maybe you have tried everything that you can to stabilize things in your life. You grasp at the proverbial straws with the hope that something will just work for you, but they do not. Stress overwhelms and before you know it everything is gone, and all you want is what you once had.

I have been there and I have laid my life out as an example of how things can go bad. I guess this book, more than anything is a story of my personal journey from the heights of happiness and success to the depths of despair and tragedy and the beginnings of my journey back.

In this journey I have worked and tried things that would bring me back to what I once thought that I had. I have had different jobs and business opportunities that I thought would help me start climbing back up the ladder of success, and then they were gone. I have learned that you cannot stop though; you must keep working and trying to better your circumstances. If one thing does not work then go for another. Be logical about it though, have a plan and a clear direction, do not do something because it sounds or looks good.

Remember people and companies are trying to get you to buy or sell their products and services. They know just the right words to say that will give you the impression that they are the ones who can and will help you out of your financial difficulties. If you do not look at things clearly you may just end up once again on a path to nowhere. Then you have lost money and tine, but you have gained experience. We need to learn and grow from our mistakes.

What I have found, looking back at things over the years, is that one thing has lead me to another. There was a clear defined path that I took with a bunch of little side trips on dead end trails. There has been a series of events that eventually lead me to where and what I'm doing today. It is hard, but the Lord will lead and guide me to the right things and the right ways. He knows best.

At times the things we want are not the things we need. We do not know or realize what would happen if we receive everything we want. We need to accept that we have become who and what we need to be at this point in the journey, but continue to grow and learn so we can be all that God created us to be. Our development depends on how we respond to life's circumstances.

We may want to get back to what we once had but that may not be the best plan. If we fully focus on what we once had in the past, we cannot move forward. If we want to move forward we need to let go of the past, it is over. We need to move boldly into our future, a bright future with new things and experiences.

If, like me, you have felt you have been in a freefall, from success to disaster, there is one more thing you need to do. I have learned this, and have begun to follow this. You have already free-fallen, and did all that you could do in your power to keep what you had but you have lost it. You may feel defeated, beaten and have no desire to move or do anything else and just do not know what to do.

There is one thing that you need to have the courage to do. That is let go, yes I said let go. Let go of the past, let go of everything that has you bound to the former things. You can no longer do what you have been doing. You cannot hang onto the past or people. You cannot go in the direction that you think is right. You need to let go and put your life and future into the hands of the Lord.

It is like being on the ledge of a burning building and the fireman is on the ground saying, "Let go, jump and we will catch you and save you." Your past life is that burning building, all that you had, your life or possessions are inside being destroyed. They are gone - your past, your hopes, and your dreams are in flames.

You may be on the ledge holding onto the past. You may want nothing more than to curl up and snuggle safely in your bed once again. It is gone, you need to realize that, accept that. You cannot hold onto it or get it back or you will be in pain and danger of burning. Let it go and have the faith that the fireman will catch you.

Let go of your past, your pain, your hardships, your hopes and dreams and lay it into the Lord's hands. He will catch you and give you what you need. The Lord will save you if you only let Him.

Are you ready to let go, free-fall once again and
put your faith in God?

Accept and say the Lord's will be done.

"Lord, heavenly Father I give up my will, the will that You gave me, and give it back to You, for I know that You will do what is right and best, and I will follow Your will and ways for I know that they are best and You will not let me fall."

Once you do this you will be relieved of pain and pressure. You will find a peace in your life, a greater peace than you have ever known. Once you have let go of the past, new ways and ideas will open up once again. It is like spring after a long cold winter. The grass will once again turn green, the leaves on the trees will open up and the flowers will once again begin to blossom. It is a great and beautiful feeling.

When you do this, you will see how the Lord has blessed you and continues to bless your life. He will help you grow and move into a new life with new successes. You will begin to live in a new future; a better future with the Lord.

The story of Job from the bible comes to mind. In short, the devil took everything from Job to test him and his faith in the Lord. I mean he took his wife, children, land, wealth, and his health. Job was in a state of nothing and just wanted to die but he did not curse or blame God for what happened to him. Because Job remained faithful to God and put his entire life into the Lord's hands, Job was blessed with more than what he had before.

We are all sinners and only have what we have by the grace of God. In the case of Job, God actually withdrew His grace, blessings and protection from Job so the devil could test him. When that grace was no longer present, all that Job had, including his health was taken away. Job was actually in the natural state of living if it were not for the grace and love of God.

Now we may not be like Job, we may not suffer how he did. We may not get back more than we did before, but we will get what we need. We will be under the blessings of the Lord and when the Lord blesses, He blesses abundantly.

There is one key to receiving the Lord's blessings, no matter what has happened. You may not know why things happened the way they did. You may understand that it is for a reason and purpose greater than us. No matter what, you need to express thankfulness to the Lord God.

Thank God for helping you and carrying you through the tough and bad times. Thank Him that things were not worse. Our thankfulness should show that in spite of the many problems that we cause for ourselves and to others, He has and continues to show us His love and grace. Our thankfulness should also be that we understand He only allows us to experience that which we can handle, nothing more that will destroy us. The Lord is great and good, His will be done.

CHAPTER TWENTY-TWO

WHAT DO WE WANT?

Now that you are on your way back to success, what is it that you want? You have let go of your past, and moved into a new future, a new life. What do you want? What do you need? Where do you want to be, how do you want to live? Once you have decided, how do you get there?

Do you want a good job or a nice home? I'm sure that is on most people's radar screen. Maybe you want to be a more loving person. Some would like to become more charitable, loving and considerate to others. Maybe you would like to advance at work, or to own your own business. The scope is limitless.

For myself, I have reached the stage of my life, where I only want enough to get my bills paid and be debt-free with savings. I want to be able to live my faith and give of my time to the Lord. I would like to help others, have a nice place to live that I can call my own, and share my life with someone special, to be able to lay back with that person and spend time together and just forget the things of this life and the world for a while. I want to raise my two boys and provide for their future and help them grow into strong, confident men.

How are we to get from where we are now to where we want to be? When I was 19 my friend Steve told us to make a list of goals for our life. We were to make a list of both short term and long term goals. I made this list, set it aside, and found it years later and well the goals that I had at 19 are different than how my life had turned out.

At 19 I wanted to get an education and a good well-paying job. I wanted to find and get married to the love of my life and spend the rest of my life with her. Also, I wanted to take multiple missionary journeys for my church. You know from reading this book that I kind of missed those goals.

There is an aggressive way to attain your goals, or to attain what you want. Go after them with every fiber of your being, think about it and do all you can to attain those goals. Strive for it at all times and let nothing get in your way. For me this is a bit too much in your face. I know it has worked for some, even for many but it sounds a bit ruthless and I do not want to be that kind of person.

I would rather change myself than change the world. I want to change my life to conform to what I want to become. Sometimes it may be easier to start at the end rather than the beginning. By this I mean take a good look at yourself, then picture what you want to become and imagine yourself as already being there, being what you want to be, doing what you want to do, having what you want.

Now I'm not talking about just lying around day dreaming of what your future will be. I mean picture yourself and what you need in order to be where you want in this life. Then remove that which does not conform to what you want. First change yourself, for more than anything we hold ourselves back from attaining what we already know we want to become.

Once you start looking at yourself as how you want to be and not how you currently are, things will begin to open up for you. You will start seeing things differently, your life will change. You will begin to get rid of things and activities that keep you from changing and growing. More than this when you get rid of that which holds you back, then you can see the things that will bring you to your destination. You start acting different and talking different. You clear your mind and you see the direction you need to go in. You begin to do what is necessary to attain your goals.

You may be tempted to try to get others to conform as well, however if you spend your time trying to change others, rather than yourself, you will be neglecting the changes you need to make in your own life. It is easier to complain or try to change others than do the hard work of changing yourself.

When you focus on changing yourself, you become a positive influence for change all around you.

When you change, people will act differently around you. Some may not like the new change and they may try to criticize and hinder you in any way they can, but don't let them. You are growing beyond where they are and becoming someone that they admire but they are unwilling to make the hard choices necessary to change. If you stay on your path, you will change and those around you will change as well.

A new life that you may have never been able to dream of will come into play. You will be happier and have a greater peace. Some may ask you what happened, what did you do, then you can tell them and help them out of their circumstances.

The one thing that I have found in my life, as long as I was focused on attaining a goal, and did not pay attention to anything else, I never attained that goal. Once I said, this is what I want, and lived my life, and did not put blinders on to that which was around me, things worked out. I have noticed this with others as well. Here is an example. When I was young I wanted to find a wife, and there was a time when that was all I focused on, with little success. I would go from relationship to relationship but nothing really came to fruition. After a while I gave up and said, "I have looked but I guess there is no one out there for me." When I stopped looking I met the person that I was to marry and a short time later I was engaged and married.

Sometimes we need to let things flow naturally, and they will happen in their own time. We need to put our ideas aside of what we think we want or need. We must put those desires into the Lord's hands with the knowledge that if it is His will He will open things up before our eyes and show us what we need and bless us with what we want.

When I met my wife, I was on a cruise with people on it from all over the country and other parts of the world. When I went over to meet the person who would become my wife, I just thought she was cute and wanted to say hi. As we spoke I found out that she was from Chicago, just like I was. We only lived about 20 miles apart. She was there getting over a relationship as well. It was the Lord who brought the two of us together at that point. During that first meeting I knew that she was going to be my wife.

The Lord will lead us in His ways and what is right and good for us. He will give us what we need and who we need and send us to others who need us. He will do what is right and good, even though we have our own ideas.

CHAPTER TWENTY-THREE

PREDESTINATION: WHAT IF I HAD DONE DIFFERENTLY?

The question, "What if I would have done things differently?" can nag at us, especially when things are not going well. We can say things and as the words leave our lips we are already regretting what we said. Once said they cannot be taken back; they can have some deep ramifications on relationships, friendships, jobs and the like.

I had a friend once who was about six years younger than me. We belonged to the same church and he had moved into the area when I was about 15. He had suffered some loss in his life and I wanted to help him out. I tried to take him under my wing, especially as he grew into his mid to late teen years. I would take him to the church youth activities and introduced him around.

As he reached his early 20s he kind of went his own way, I did not see him much after that. He drifted away from church and the church activities.

One night I had a dream that he was killed in a car accident. This dream was specific; it showed the day of the week, how the accident happened, what time it happened and what was going on at church at the time. I awoke; this disturbed me. I thought about this often, and wanted to tell him about it, but I rarely saw him. One day I called him aside and I told him about the dream. I warned him what may happen and when. He kind of blew me off and said that there was nothing that he could do if that is how it was to be.

About nine months later I got a phone call in the middle of the night from my father who told me that this young man was killed in a car accident. It had happened earlier that night, the same night of the week that I had dreamed. The accident took place just as I had dreamed, and the same activities were going on at church as I had dreamed.

Could he have changed his future? Was my dream a warning to him? Could he have changed his future if rather than blowing me off, he had taken a different action? We do not know.

I do not believe in predestination; our lives are in our hands, but I do believe that there is a course we are to be on. It is our choice if we follow that path or not. Life is a series of choices and decisions, each one is ours to make, and we come under the consequences of every decision every day. How much our choices affect our future, I cannot say. Every choice that we make has consequences and consequences affect future choices and decisions that we make and on and on it goes. Will it or can it change our ultimate destiny?

We don't know what would have happened if we had made a different choice unless God shows us. Life does not have a rewind button. Once we do something it cannot be changed or modified. So we wonder. All we have is hindsight and we can look at and analyze the consequences of each of our decisions. This I have done many times.

As I'm sure you know I have thought much about this especially when it comes to my trip to Montana. What if I would have followed my instincts, decided to eat the cost of the airline ticket, and decided not to go to Montana? I guess I would be a different person in a way. How did the accident influence other decisions I've made since then? How did it affect the lives of others?

There is one event in my life that I know for sure had deep enough ramifications that it would have really changed the course of my life had I chosen a different path: my first engagement. Besides the financial hardships caused by that experience, the main thing is that if I would not have met and been engaged to this first girl there is a good chance that I would not have met the woman who became my wife.

I believe that we can change our future. Each decision will give us a new set of circumstances and outcomes that will lead us to a new set of choices and outcomes. The only difference is what takes place between the beginning and the end, which is what we have power over. The Lord will lead us in the best direction if we allow Him.

If I would have made different choices, I may have still met my wife, but under completely different circumstances. If I would not have gone to Montana, I would have learned and grown as I needed to under different conditions, maybe better, maybe worse. The game plan for our lives changes every day not only because of the choices and decisions that we make but also the choices and decisions that others make.

Though we have a free will and some control over our lives, our lives are also influenced by the choices and decisions of those around us. Our lives can change in an instant depending on the decision of some ruler or dictator or president from the other side of the world. All we can do is put things in the Lord's hands and follow His path, for He knows what is right and will bless us accordingly.

All that being said, along with all that I have told you in this book about what I have lived though, I'm happy that things worked out as they did because it is those experiences, hardships, pain, sorrow, and joy that have made me what I am today. I love my two boys, I still care about my ex-wife. I have a friendship and concern for my ex-fiancé, I feel a special connection and bond to those who I was in the accident with in Montana. All in all I'm a better person because of what I have gone though in life, and you have only had a glimpse of what I have lived though.

CHAPTER TWENTY-FOUR

WHAT IS YOUR FOCUS?

I have touched on this a few times in this book, "What is your focus?" Do you only look at your needs and wants and shove the needs of others to the side? Are you focused so much on past hurts, losses, and pain that you are unwilling or unable to move forward in your life? Are you so focused on your problems that you are unable to see that which is around you clearly, unable to clearly see choices make sound decisions? Maybe you are so focused on money and transitory goods that you are unable to see or feel the love of family and friends.

When we become too focused on our problems, that is all that we see. Anything that is to the left or the right we miss, because we are looking at this one thing. When we are too focused on one thing, we miss things, good things. We may not understand the reasons why what we want is not coming to us, Because we are so focused on attaining it, the ultimate prize, we do not see the problems in achieving it.

When I was in the commercial real estate field, there were times when I would be so focused on the end of a transaction, earning the big commission that I would miss things in the deal, or not see the danger signs that the deal would not come to fruition.

The problem was that I had made mistakes in my personal life. I had obligated myself to more debt than I could pay for, mostly with my house. Because of this heavy debt load, I was short on cash and had my creditors calling me both at work and at home. I knew that if I could just make this one deal, the commission would be large enough to pay off my creditors and make my house payments until my next deal came in.

I would be working on deals for months with a potential commission of over $50,000.00 to $100,000.00. If you get two of these a year you are in pretty good shape, and I was working on a few of them every year. When you are in a commission based business it is like being a gambler, dreaming of the big score. It is always about the next big deal, you live on the hope that you will be dealt 4 aces in the next hand. It perverts your whole way of thinking. You become so focused on what can be that you lose sight of reality. This is especially true when you make financial decisions based on bad assumptions of the next big deal coming in.

I was good at what I did; at least I thought I was better than what I was. I would start the year and when the market picked up in late winter or early spring I would have two or three of these big deals lining up. I would begin to think that I was in for a banner year, making close to $200,000.00. I would make myself believe that this was the fact, before any of the deals were even close to working out. I would believe that I had already earned the commission, but the commission was not even close to being earned. I was the biggest fool of all, because I fooled myself.

In this state of mind you begin working for the commission. Once you have made your future financial commitments based on the false assumption of earning that big pay out, you just need to earn that money or you will be in deep trouble. Actually you are in deep trouble and just don't realize it at the time. You need that money, you need that commission, and you need the deal to close so you will be paid. Then you become so consumed with the end point of being given that big check, that you do not want to see problems or potential problems. You do not want to know or recognize that there could even be a problem because you need that commission, and you need it now.

There were times when we had a building selected and put in an offer; the owners accepted the offer and contracts were being prepared. Problems would arise, and the purchaser would express concern. They may even indicate that they would be interested in a different building. I would look but I would keep pressing for the original building because I was only concerned with what I needed – that commission. Before long the other problems were found and the whole deal would fall apart.

When this happened, I would wonder why? Why was it that I had been given this opportunity for this huge commission that could take care of my financial commitments and then have it fall apart? Then I would be left with nothing, or even less than nothing. I would question the Lord, I would place the blame on buyers or sellers because the transaction did not work out. If it only had worked things would be so much better. I would not be in this situation.

I would look everywhere and place the blame, except where the responsibility laid, with me, my attitude, and my wrong focus on the gain rather than completing the transaction and serving the customer. The problem also was with me, for obligating myself financially based on income that I did not earn, did not have, and may never have.

There are times when we can become so focused on what we want, what we need, and what we think we deserve that we lose sight of reality. We put our needs and wants over others, especially those that we depend on to receive what we want or need. In some cases someone may owe us money or promised to give us something and when we do not receive it, as promised, we become angry with them. We question why did you not give me what I need, what I want or what you owe me? Friendships and relationships can be lost over this. Because we are so focused on what we want, we fail to see or understand why they could not give us what they owe us or what they promised to give us.

On the other side, we cannot become so focused on ourselves and keeping what we have that we fail to live up to our obligations to others. If we do not have something or cannot do something we cannot promise our time, abilities or anything to others that we do not have. If we expect to have it, we still cannot promise it to others. If you only do and promise that which you can reasonably do or give, you will not disappoint others when you cannot deliver that which you promised. I promised things to my family and my creditors that I could not deliver. I caused disappointment and debt. Everyone would have been much better off if I had not promised or committed myself and not delivered.

In the past when I have committed myself to debt, I made promises that I had every intention of keeping, but because of situations I could not. I would question why the Lord does not help me, why does He give me the opportunity to earn all this money and then pull the rug out from underneath me and leave me dangling in the wind of debt.

What I did not see is that the Lord was blessing me; He was giving me opportunity to succeed, to fulfill my obligations, to support my family, and to pay my debt, the debt that I had at the time. It was me who increased my debt. It was me and my actions that caused what the Lord had set before me at work to fall apart and I ended up with nothing. It was not the will of God, it was not the buyers or the sellers who destroyed my opportunities; it was myself, no one or nothing else. I refused to take responsibility for my actions so I was doomed to repeat them time and time again until I reached rock bottom. It was only then that I began looking back at my life and saw the many mistakes that I have made, including the shortcuts to prosperity that I tried to make. Only then did I see all the pain that I had caused for myself and others because of my attitudes and not dealing in reality. It is because of me that I'm no longer married, that I do not live with my kids, that I no longer own a business and that I no longer have a home to call my own.

Take the time to look at yourself. Take a look at your actions and your responses. Look at your attitude. Look at where you are and where you could be if you had done things differently. Honestly assess your life and yourself and see why things are the way they are. What is your responsibility for your situation? What you do you need to change, what you can change about yourself to make you, your family and your future better? Do this now, don't be like me and wait until everything is gone.

CHAPTER TWENTY-FIVE

YES YOU CAN

I know this is a bit trite, but it is true, we shy away from work, or doing things that seem hard. Our mind will put obstacles in our way to stop us from doing things that seem hard or those we are unsure about doing.

I can't find a job; the job market is tough right now. How many of us have used this excuse when they are out of work and we reach what we believe is a wall stopping us from finding work. In fact there is work out there, some kind of work, but we do not want to do it. Maybe we believe it is beneath us or it is too hard for us to do. Someone will do this job and make money doing it, why not you?

Come on now, you may have a family to take care of. You have yourself to take care of. You need to survive and get a job, go and do it. Excuses will not feed you or your family.

This goes far beyond looking for a job, this goes into many aspects of your life. We all have dreams, things that we would like to do. What stops us from fulfilling those dreams, in most cases it is ourselves. Many times it is our own ideas, our own self-imposed obstacles that stop us from succeeding in life. Don't convince yourself that you cannot do something. You can do it. We tell ourselves we are not smart enough, that we are not strong enough and that we just cannot do it, you can and you will.

I never thought a year ago or even six months ago that I would write a book. I didn't think I could. Sure, I published a blog for a while, and I thought of writing a book then; I should have, but convinced myself that it would be too hard, that I could not write something that involved. I did not have that much to say, but here I am. The Lord arranged things in my life where this became possible. I always could have done it, but my own ideas stopped me from even trying.

We also often hear, "where there is a will, there is a way" This again is very true, you can do it. We were all born with a multitude of gifts and abilities, with everything that we need to use and succeed in life. I mean everyone, not just a few special people. You are as good, as smart, and as talented as anyone else out there. You are as they are; you can achieve what you want, what you dream about. You can do it.

Ask yourself, what is stopping me? Why don't I go out and do it? Why don't I or why can't I find a job? Ask yourself why, what self-imposed obstacles are stopping me from fulfilling my dreams and aspirations? Ask yourself why you are letting your problems and difficulties get you down. Ask yourself why do you let others control your life? Why do you let yourself be used by others to fulfill their dreams and not use your own talents and abilities to fulfill your dreams?

Why are you not moving on with your life? Why do you keep moving in the same circle of pain and sorrow? You were not meant for this, you are more than this. You can do it.

Just look at what people have achieved through history. Look at where we were one hundred years ago. Two hundred years ago, doctors still believed in bloodletting as a cure for all diseases, now look at where modern medicine is. We still have not even scratched the surface of where we will be even ten to twenty years from now.

Now I'm not that old; I was born in 1965. We live in a completely different world than the one that I was born into. Look at what we have achieved in the past forty years.

Look at all that has been achieved since man's creation, since the day that we first crawled out of the primordial soup. Did you notice that, I mixed theories here, creationism with the theory of evolution? I believe that both are true. I do not believe the God said Let it be and poof, humans and the creation just came into existence. We know that the earth, the universe and humans have been here more than 7,000 + years. I also know that there were too many chances and coincidences that things came together just by chance; there are too many holes in the evolution theory when you really look at it, to make it true. What does work though is that gods hand was involved in bringing things together and making them work in just the right way that we can into being. Who are we to decided that God worked in this way or that way, that things just appeared on the earth rather than the right chemicals amino acids came together to create life.

This is one way in which peoples thinking stops them from learning and growing. There are two main sides in this debate, those that believe that humans just evolved from nothing just by chance and those who believe that God just made them appear on the earth. The two are diametrically opposed to each other, rather than finding common ground and working together for each other's betterment. Each ones thought process is stopping then from learning and understanding life as we know it. Just look at how much time and money each side wastes trying to disprove the other side. Consider how much energy is put into fighting and arguing. Each side has made up their mind that what they believe is the only right way and that there is no other way besides what they feel or believe.

Look at how much man has achieved since the beginning. That is because we were created with innate capabilities and with the ability to achieve greatness. Some may be born with more opportunity than others, but that does not stop or limit on what you can and will achieve. You may feel that you were given a "raw deal" with your upbringing and opportunity but that is because you did not need the greater benefits to achieve and to grow. God knew that you could still achieve in spite of your "raw deal." You did not need the special chances and upbringing. You can do it.

Remember the only thing that can stop you in life is you yourself. Don't let this happen. Follow your dreams, make them real, it may take time, but you can do it. I'm not saying to drop everything in your life and run off to join the circus, but if that is your dream, grow into it, begin to make it real in your life.

As with anything to make your dreams real they have to be worked for, they will not just appear. As you follow your dreams there must be order, do not close off what you are doing now and just jump into your dream.

For me to begin writing this book there was an order of events in my life that took place, as I have written. Everything that has happened has led me to this point, every detail. Before I went into blogging I was looking for a new job, there were a series of events and recommendations from friends and relatives that let me to different social networks to assist in finding a job. Once I got more involved in Twitter and LinkedIn, I came in contact with bloggers, read what they had to say and decided to start my own blog.

Of course when I started writing the blog I thought that it would be easy money, that the readers would magically appear along with the advertisers and I would begin to make money. If I would have quite my other job, and just gone into blogging I would have been in great trouble, for the money did not roll in like I once believed. Little did I know at the time that blogging was just another step in the process to lead me to where I am now, writing a book. What is next, is to be seen, it is in the Lord's Hands for He knows what is best and right.

CHAPTER TWENTY-SIX

HOW TO SUCCEED

So you want to find success in your life? I have gone through in detail how not to succeed, but what is the way to succeed, to get ahead? I cannot guarantee that you will become rich, or get everything that you want out of life, but I will give you some insight.

Before we start, if you have gone through a series of problems in your life, you need to get your head on straight. After a period of going through the problems that I have gone through you may become strange, odd, a bit different, or a bit off. It is hard to explain. Perhaps it is kind of paranoia because you have been hurt and suffered but it will be hard to get ahead unless you deal with this first.

You will need to move on with your life and leave the past behind. You will need to get out and meet and spend time with other people. Do not lock yourself away and separate from others, social contact is a must. You will also need to learn to trust others once again. It will be hard, but do it. Take it slow, but learn to trust and accept. Once you have done this then you can begin to move forward.

The first thing that we need to be a success in life is to treat others with honesty and integrity. What can hold us back and not treat others as they should be treated is what we have discussed in this book - people want things now. They try to take the shortest route that they can find to get what they want. As I have written, I did not do this, and see where I ended up. You will find that the path that looks like it is lined with gold is not. If someone is dangling a sure thing or a quick way to get rich, run the other way.

We all want an easy path to success, wealth, and money. There are plenty of people out there that are more than willing to satisfy that need. They will promise you things make the future sound so great and wonderful that you just have to listen to them. Go ahead, do what they say, follow their instructions to quick wealth. They are the ones that will get the money, and as for you, well they could care less.

I'm not just talking about the scam artists, but in all things take the time to do things right. I mentioned this back when I was writing about attitudes. Do things right, do not try to scam your way around with as little work as possible. If you have to do a little extra, spend a bit more time do it. I cannot say this enough. I know there are times where we really need the money and it is hard not to grab on and go for it. As the old saying goes, if it looks too good to be true, it is.

Using this book writing process as an example, I finished this book, at least I thought I did, and a friend of mine, Christine, pushed me to read and edit it three more times. I will insert here that I dislike rereading my work over and over. The easy route would have been to say I have done this and I'm finished and that is it. I want to get this off to some publishers and find out what their opinion is. I sucked it up and read it again, made changes and added to the book. I could have stopped there, but I followed what she said and read it again, made more changes and again and made more. I figured that I was done and sent it off to a few publishers and now I'm writing this, what I think is my final chapter. If I would have stopped two weeks ago, the book would not have been as good as what it is now.

Do what is needed; take the time to do a bit extra. Get things right, you will be better off in the end. As I began to research publishers, my eyes were opened to just the amount of work that needed to be done to get my book published. I thought that all I needed to do is send my book off to them and they either accepted or rejected it. Yes, there are some who will do this, but others will ask for more. You don't send your manuscript; actually you put together documents telling about the book and examples of what is in your book. This means more writing and more time spent until I can get published. Beyond this there is more work and writing that needs to be done, you need to begin your marketing process, find outlets, blogs and other websites that are willing to sell your book for you. To do it right you need to also write marketing packets and submit it to the publishers as well. Then if you really want to do things right you need to find a literary agent to go to the publishers as a representative.

So what to do, go for the quick payout or do all of this extra work and receive a potential better return in the end? There are other options, I could self-publish and just sell eBooks through my contacts. With this I could earn some quick money but since my exposure is less, in the end I wouldn't earn as much. Yes, I could earn 100% of the sales, but not sell as many. Or I could go through the extra work and go to a full publishing house, where they will keep the majority of the sales, but I will have the potential to sell a greater quantity of books.

What to do? I need the money now, but if I go for the quick payout I could lose out on so much more in the future. I decided to go with the longer harder process and bet on the bigger return. If that does not work out I can fall back on the self-publishing.

Remember we get paid for our work and labor. We go to work every day and we get paid either a salary or an hourly wage in exchange of giving our time and labor. The more time and energy you give the more you will receive. If you want to earn more money, you need to work longer and harder. I found this out in the real estate business. People see real estate agents and the big commissions that they can earn and think that it is a nice and easy job. It is not. Sure you can earn the big payout, but if you want to earn the big money it takes a lot of time and energy.

The largest commission that I earned while selling real estate was $200,000.00. That looks great. You show a building do a little work and go to a closing table and get a check for all that money. Not quite. To earn that money it took over a year or two of work and multiple years of relationship building before that. It took marketing money and hours upon hours of background work that no one ever sees. On top of this you need to figure all the work that you had to put in on some transactions that did not work out and of course you did not receive any income for all the work that you did. I mean late nights and early mornings. You can put in hours upon hours of work and have nothing to show for it in the end. If you want the big payout, you need to put in the time and energy; you need to do the work.

The Lord will bless your labor; you will find a success in your life. Stay the right course, change your attitudes, do a little extra, work hard, be the best that you can be and you will receive your reward.

If I would have put the same passion and work in trying to find a new, good job a few years ago, as I have with this book, my life could be different now. Back when I was losing my business and my life began to fall apart, I was overwhelmed with problems and could not make clear decisions or even think about what needed to be done. There were cover letters and resume improvements that I could have made, but did not. I could not figure out where to start or how to even write a good cover letter. I was unable to make clear decisions, the old 'what if' was plaguing my mind. I had no idea how to start the process or what to write. I would make applications through a few job websites and call it a day. No cover letter or a bad one and a very bad resume.

Things have changed since then, my mind has cleared out and I can think. I'm no longer acting and making decisions out of fear of the future and fear of making the wrong decisions. I have put my future into the Lords hands, not mine. By doing this a great burden has been lifted for I know that He will lead and guide me down the right path.

Does my future lay with the sales of this book? Maybe it does or maybe it does not. That is still to be seen. What the writing of this book has done is helped me gain closure in my life. All the problems and difficulties that I lived under in the past are now over and part of an old life that no longer exists. I have removed them from my life and now look to a bright future. Always look forward. Leave the past in the past, our lives are in the future not the past.

What is in my future that is to be seen? Will I once again have a home of my own, and get married again? That is in the Lord's hands. I know that I would like to have my own place and I will work for that. Will I develop a relationship with a woman that I like? That is all up to the Lord. I see what I have now and realize that I have been truly blessed. I have two great sons that I love and miss dearly. I have a warm bed at night and food to eat. Beyond this I know that I have a bright and glorious future for the blessings of the Lord are upon me, He knows and does what is good and right. The blessings of the Lord are great and abundant; we all can have a bright and glorious future.

CHAPTER TWENTY-SEVEN

A FINAL WORD

When we look at children, they are full of amazement, hopes, and dreams, the same as we were when we were young. As we grow something happens. Life throws us curve balls. We no longer find the same joy and amazement in things, we become hardened and skeptical. The many hopes and dreams that we had may not have worked out. This happens to some a lesser extent and to others much greater. The more that this happens in life we begin to withdraw into ourselves, build walls around our heart, and close off the outside so we no longer can be hurt or suffer the pain. We will then no longer have dreams; we will just live each day in the hopes that things will not get any worse.

I went through this, waking every morning wondering what was going to happen next in my life, what new problem or pain was I going to go through today. I became very negative for myself and my future. I would look and see others being happy and joyful with their families, earning money and taking vacations to other places around the world. I would think why could this not be me? Why do they have all that they want? They are living the life that I wanted, but here I sit, broke, no wife, and not living with my kids. I would think back to the happier times, the vacations that we took together, the times we had together, and the pain of the loss would rise up once again. I had no joy in life, much less any happiness about myself and things around me. I would have my kids for a night or a weekend and things were good, but after I took them back home and they were no longer with me a great sadness would overwhelm me.

I would also be continually haunted by memories, not only of the good times, but memories of the time when I was going through the process of the dismantling of my life. Memories of working 75 hours a week to try to keep my house and family, of working every day for two or three weeks straight. Memories of being so tired as I worked over night that I would be like a robot.

When I worked overnight, I worked in multiple grocery stores around the area as a retail merchandiser. For a while, long after that period of my life was over, I would pass by one of those stores and all the memories and pain would well up once again, like I was still living the nightmare. The pain and loss was just as real as it had just happened yesterday. This continued on for a couple of years after the terrible events that I had gone though.

Then one day it happened, I went past one of those places that I had worked at, and it no longer was a nightmare, it was just a memory of things that had happened. Over time even these memories have faded and the pain from them no longer haunts me. This is a good thing that happens as we slowly begin to stop living in the past and start moving on with our life.

One of my children now lives with me, and I want so much more for both of my sons. I want to spend time with them and help them in any way that I can. At this time my current income does not allow me to do much for them. It hurts me because I have missed so much. It hurts me because I have hurt them and my ex. I know this time will pass and things will be better tomorrow; if not tomorrow the next day. We just need to keep on trying each day to find that nugget of gold in our life. I know that it will happen. I will get a better paying job, I will find new opportunities in my life. I have begun to dream of something better; joy is returning along with happiness.

The past is the past and that is where it should be left. We need to look to the future, build new hopes and dreams just as we did when we were children. We must find amazement and joy in the little things in life and not surround ourselves with darkness and sorrow.

Looking back on the time that I was in the depths of sorrow and feeling the pain of loss, I was drawn to that which was depressing. Even the television shows that I watched were depressing. They were dealing with other people's problems, loss, and sorrow. If I wasn't watching that I was fixated on reruns of shows that I used to watch with my family that would bring back that same old feeling of pain and loss.

Things are different now. I do not want to watch shows dealing with other people's problems and loss, but I want to watch things and be involved in things that bring about joy, hope and happiness. I no longer want to surround myself with the negative in life, but the positive. I'm done with all that. There are little things each day that can bring us joy, they are there all the time, we just have to open our eyes and look for them.

I know that I'm now a better person than I was before all the events I mentioned took place. I know that it was the Lord that led me through this dark time. My faith in Him has grown tremendously. I know that everything good comes from Him, and not through my own actions. I'm nothing without the Lord and He is the giver of all gifts and blessings. Even though it ended in disaster, I'm thankful for my marriage for without that I would not have the greatest joy in my life, my two sons.

I now have a deeper care and love for others, what they experience and go though in life. I'm no longer judgmental of others. One of the greatest outcomes of my many years of problems is growing in this love of both God and others. I have learned that our main function, our meaning of life, is love. The entire teaching of the Lord and the Ten Commandments were summed up in just a few words, "Love the Lord your God with all your heart, soul and mind, and love your neighbor as yourself." This was the central focus of Jesus' teaching. Think about this for a second, the Love of God and love of others. If we do this we will fulfill all Ten Commandments.

- We will put God first in all things and worship no others.
- We will not use His name in vain.
- We will remember the Sabbath day and keep it holy.
- We will honor our parents
- We will not kill others

- We will not commit adultery or cheat on our spouse
- We will not steal things from others
- We will not bring false witness, spread rumors, or tell lies about others
- We will not seek or dream of getting possession of other people's wife or goods.

All too many times we focus on sin rather than focusing on love. We can spend much energy focusing on our own sin and trying not to commit it. I will say this, sin does not matter; do not become fixated on it. We all sin and we will always sin. That is why the Lord Jesus gave His life on the cross, so our sins could be forgiven. Do not become obsessed with sin, all our sins can be washed away. Live your life and do what you need to do. Rather than looking at sin, focus on growing in love. If we grow in love we will not commit the sins. We will Love and follow God and we will not intentionally bring harm to others.

When people focus on sin, more often than not they focus on the sins of others, or what they perceive as sins that others commit. This is completely wrong and contrary to the teaching of the Lord Jesus. This is not showing Love, but being a judge over others and over sin itself. There is no one who can judge other than the Lord God. So in fact when we do this we are breaking the commandment of Jesus to love in all aspects. We are not showing our love for others because we are judging them. Likewise we are not showing our love for God, because we are putting ourselves equal to God in our judgment of sin.

Jesus also spoke about the judgment of others, and comparing yourself to them. We will often do this in order to make ourselves feel better about our own faults and failings. Jesus said, "Do not look at the sliver in your brother's eye, and miss the beam in your own eye." Here he was telling us not to judge others for their sin and their failings, because each of us have our own sin to deal with.

In everything we do, we must act from a place of love.

- Duty without love makes one resentful

- Justice without love makes one cruel
- Truth without love makes one judgmental
- An upbringing without love makes one crafty
- Intellect without love makes one sly
- Friendliness without love makes one hypocritical
- Ability without love makes one uncompromising
- Responsibility without love makes one dictatorial
- Honor without love makes one indifferent
- Wealth without love makes one selfish
- Faith without love makes one fanatical.
- How do you live, how can you live without love.

Don't be critical or judgmental in life, show love and compassion, you do not know the problems that others face or why they do things. Refrain from anger and show grace, for the Lord God has shown you grace as well. Put everything in His hands, and things will be done right according to His will and way. We are nothing in comparison to the might, power, and love of God our Heavenly Father.

If we put our faith in God with the knowledge that things will work out right by His hand, we will begin to see life from a new and better prospective. What seemed so tragic at the time will be less tragic and stressful. He will always do what is right and we will be better off for it in the end. The Lord will provide.

Prayer

I will survive, I will get back on my feet, and I will be in a better position than I was before. With the Lord all things are possible and my faith and trust is solely in him. The Lord never gives me more than I can handle; He will see me through my dark days. He is there for me, I will grasp His hand and follow His lead.

~

We can do this, we will do this.

Manufactured by Amazon.ca
Bolton, ON

29673716R00088